# *Tales from an Actor's Life*

# steven
# BERKOFF

*Tales from an Actor's Life*

**The Robson Press**

First published in Great Britain in 20
The Robson Press
an imprint of Biteback Publishing Ltd
Westminster Tower
3 Albert Embankment
London SE1 7SP
Copyright © Steven Berkoff 2011

Steven Berkoff has asserted his rights under the Copyright, Designs and
Patents Act 1988 to be identified as the author of this work.

ISBN 978-1-84954-173-2

10 9 8 7 6 5 4 3 2 1

A CIP catalogue record for this book is
available from the British Library.

Set in Caslon by Namkwan Cho
Cover design by Namkwan Cho

Printed and bound by
CPI Group (UK) Ltd, Croydon, CR0 4YY.

# CONTENTS

Introduction    vii

The Beginning of Joseph K.    1

Goin' Bowling Tonight, Eddie?    13

Lincoln – A Provincial Rep    25

Take-Over    35

A Crap Job    43

A Remote Rep Company    61

Titus!    71

The One    77

An Unusual Audition    97

The Arts Lab, Drury Lane    113

Instinct    123

You're a Film Actor!    133

On the Set    143

Waiting    153

Funny How it Starts    165

Steven Berkoff Talks to Kirk Douglas    175

Time    185

The Actor's Life    195

# INTRODUCTION

*O*f course it goes without saying that a writer paddles around in his own little pond when seeking some interesting winkle of information for a new work, and since these tales are not meant to be altogether biographical, some have been stretched and embellished. However, the core, the bedrock must ultimately be oneself. This is where we begin. All these tales are basically true stories and have been lived and enjoyed or suffered by me, the actor.

They are stories moreover that all actors will identify with and in many cases have experienced, but they are also for anyone who has struggled to express themselves on any level and has had to deal with the not always pleasant fact that your good fortunes will often depend on others, who may not always be well disposed towards you.

*What a bizarre world is theatre since such a protean art form has no fixed rules by which to abide but is subject to the will, desires and tastes of whoever happens to be in the driving seat, whether agents, directors, writers or even producers. All will have a turn in making their voice heard, believing that he who shouts the loudest will hold sway. And as for the actor, against these swirling tides of opinions he or she swims, braving the surge, plunging into the roaring foam, they must battle to reach the sanctuary of the shore and even then, exhausted, panting for breath, merely glad to be alive, they are subjected to the darts of the critics.*

*Acting must be one of the strangest of professions since the rules are so flexible and few can agree even on the simplest of them, so the actor must struggle and decide for himself which route to take. For the cynic, acting is about being heard and not bumping into the furniture. An actor colleague of mine, who incidentally is a superb performer, calls his work 'shouting at night'. Some directors love to pontificate about iambic pentameters and keeping to the metre, even when it makes little sense of the text, while others will instruct you to 'feel' the verse. Some directors love to get to work immediately and block the play so you are plunged into it immediately which is what actors need, while others will gather the cast round a table and discuss it until the actors' spirits are dried up and stifled.*

*However, there is a camaraderie amongst actors that is quite rare in other performing arts since what they are basically doing is unravelling their lives in front of you. How they need and feed off each other depends on the exact word that will send them on their way, like passing the baton.*

*After a while, the actors in a play gradually cohere and become a family, living together, depending on each other, weeping in grief at the ultimate dissolution of the family on the last night, swearing to remain faithful friends for life and paradoxically, rarely meeting again! But what nearly all actors have in common is an inordinate desire to please the audience, a terrible hunger for their approval and most of all their love. An insecure actor on the stage, hearing some laughter of acknowledgement for an inflection he placed on a word or for a piece of physical timing will suddenly grow in dimension, will swell with pride and all fears will be gone.*

*'Oh what a piece of work is man.'*

# 1.

# THE BEGINNING OF JOSEPH K.

Goddam it was tough! And it's something he wanted to do, wanted to do so badly he could feel the need almost leaking out of his bones. To be more than what he was, to be more than what he had been, which was a part-time actor fluttering like crows that hover over decayed rubbish hoping to pick up a mouldy scrap here and there. No doubt some of the work had been nourishing and he had learnt much in those lean times when he managed to get a one-off gig at a respectable rep company. But most times, it was just a few lines in some shoddy TV play that he was so happy to have. At least he was working, was getting on the tube to the BBC in White City, walking up to the long reception desk and giving his name and then being told to go to the third floor and meeting the director. He'd knock and enter, be introduced by the assistant and have a brief chat. How enviously busy the director looked, surrounded by phones and scripts, plans of sets, coloured charts on the wall, pretty secretaries typing away furiously. The TV directors always looked dynamic, always sure of themselves and radiated a healthy positive energy as if they fed like wild beasts on the flesh of others, the writers, the assistants, the producers, all who were under their powerful paws and ready to be devoured at their wish. And what were the actors but mere aperitifs that they could swallow down wholesale, like oysters, their sallow, soft, needy flesh offering little resistance.

The director sat behind his desk, his eyes glittering and examining you like a grand gourmet in a restaurant casually examines the menu. And what are you exactly? Not a bold filet mignon, or steak tartare, more a small hors d'oeuvre of chopped liver perhaps. The actor felt the power of the great lion overwhelm him but tried to stay calm and focused and not look as he felt. Not look as he really felt, which was a threadbare and low order of beast, a casual actor, just one of those carrion crows that feast on what others have left behind. He could not help but compare his own life with this buzzing hive of industry, an office full of creative dynamics, a seething muscular operation in the process of creating a mighty production that would be seen by millions. Everything in the great beast's office seemed to threaten the actor's whole existence. His small rented semi-basement flat in Pimlico, with its tiny kitchen just off the living area. At a desk by the window, from which he looked up at the passers-by, he would sit and calmly wait for the phone to ring and while waiting seek to fulfil the reason why God gave him valuable space on earth, while others, far more worthy, had their breath snatched from them by disease, warfare, or the tragic spectacle of being spread-eagled on the road, the result of some drunken sod in a car. "But here … You mister … have life," he told himself. "Seize it! Seize it God damn you and don't just fritter it away! No! No!" He mustn't do that and so after making his umpteenth cup of tea he sat by his modest wooden desk, his typewriter in front of him, and made an attempt to excite his brain enough to send spiralling down to his fingers marvellous words. Wondrous images.

But so far, not much… Not too much and so it might be time for another cup of tea or maybe he would ring an old friend who had been known to while away the time with him since she too, was in a bit of a quandary of how she could make use of this incredible universe and this miraculous gift of life. She, like him, had trained, if that's not too ambitious a word for the back-street academy they had attended, but trained to be an actress and had left full of ambition and fluffy dreams, a spotless unlined face shunted out into the world that was already saturated with these half-baked wannabes. Like him, she had dutifully rolled out her bits of Ibsen, her tired reams of Chekhov, and her over-cooked Tennessee Williams. But it was reject, reject, reject all the way.

They sat in the stalls, these Oxbridge mandarins only half-listening, eyes glazing over as yet another poor applicant stood pathetically before them trailing their dreams and ambitions like worn-out old rags. Then after the usual, "Thank you very much, we'll…" the actors gathered up their shredded fantasies and walked off the stage and then waited for days and sometimes for weeks for the agent to call and say: "Darling, they loved you and want to offer you…" but it was seldom, if ever, to be. And just as the stars naturally gravitate to their own kind and love being seen with each other grinning and gurning on the red carpets of the world, well, so do the rejected ones, the sad ones, the helpless ones yearn for each other's company to console and soothe each other and to fan the ever-diminishing flame that one day they hope will become an inferno of success but which for now is just a small gentle flame, but at least it is still alight... Just.

But! Something had changed... yes, something had definitely changed and it started like one of those quirks of fate where the stimulus comes from outside and not from anything one laboriously struggles and works at, since by one's nature it is always the same path that is trod – the same thoughts and the same dreary patterns. Fate occasionally throws something new into the spokes and the consequent wobble might offer all sorts of new inroads.

And so it was that his good friend Wesley, of Irish descent and a person of infinite charm and humour rang him one day to ask if he could temporarily take his acting class for him in some remote part of West London, which he said he would since he had done a course in mime and did have some unusual physical dexterity; unusual when compared to the modest skills of actors who were currently shouting from London's stages at night. So he travelled to the far western suburbs of London, and found the little school and a small eager group of students sitting around and waiting passively to be entertained by the replacement teacher. Our neophyte teacher was having none of that and he quickly got them up and using their bodies. He did the required two hours and the head of the school seemed much taken with the actor's technique. The actor was so excited, so overcome with his first-ever class, his first time teaching that he conveyed all this to Wesley like it was the coming revelation.

And now, instead of bombarding every repertory company with pleading letters looking for acting work which might just as well have been confetti scattered hither and thither in the wind, he now offered his services as a professional teacher to the first-rate drama schools. And lo and behold, he received a positive response from his old drama school that he thought it might be wise to apply to. It was almost a decade since the actor had left that establishment and there was a new, younger and more vital guvnor at the helm who seemed most interested in what he had to offer and suggested that he might like to direct an actual work that made full use of his movement and mime techniques!

To direct! To be responsible for creating work, for directing a group of smart and eager students, to use every cell of his lately severely underused brain, to be a true professional, a teacher, adviser, creator. Oh my God how wonderful, how simply unbelievably brilliant to be at last tested, tried and not found wanting. How marvellous is that? Even within his body he felt a strange and sudden swelling up, not just of pride but as if his body so starved, so undernourished was being revived, replenished as if his organs were sucking his dreams out of the very ether.

But what, what play, what work could he introduce to the class where he could put himself at the helm and sail to hitherto unchartered waters and reveal sights never before seen? Alas, now that the euphoria had died down, now that the sheer excitement of his elevated position had been replaced by the practicalities, he found that his mind was now a seething nest of doubts. There are thousands of plays, countless dramas but which one to pick that would be the perfect vehicle to display his talents, his mind, his peculiar and singular way of seeing things. Which one! He decided to take his anguish, his seething cauldron of snakes to the benign head of the small academy and confess his quandary, his torment, but not so much that the guvnor might be tempted to say: "Well if you do find it so very difficult and you wouldn't be the first one to do so, perhaps you should relinquish the post and come back when you feel more settled." That would be just the very last thing in the world that he wanted. He explained his predicament as a challenge and that he was so desperately keen to serve his boss and, of course, the students with as exciting a theme as possible. The headman of the school looked at him slightly quizzically and said: "Look, my dear boy, we're not looking for the greatest piece of theatre there has ever been but merely a vehicle for the class. There are twelve students in the class and it would be of the greatest benefit to them if each could be involved. It's about them. They want to be stretched. They also want to be inspired and excited. And if you can't find a play for twelve persons, look elsewhere. Last year they did their Shakespeare and now you need to look towards a contemporary theme. That's all. That's all you have to do. It can be anything as long as it involves them all since most are paying a substantial sum of money and we want to make sure they can each express themselves and learn the art of performance. It doesn't even have to be a play if you can't find what you're looking for. You might adapt something, improvise. Make them use their imaginations."

The young and future director nodded and nodded with relief as if he was nodding away the little demons that had invaded his head. He nodded, he felt better, reassured, by the way the man spoke to him in such a calm, friendly fashion. It felt good just to be in the room with him. Suddenly, he knew why he felt so much better. The man was talking to him in a way that his own father could never bring himself to do. No, not ever. And didn't he need that solace that came from the wisdom that only an older man can give? It was like sweet rain that waters the sapling tree and nourishes it and prepares it to withstand fierce winds and bitter frost. But alas, he had none of it and so scooped up dirty puddles of water from wherever he could – the rancid brackish water that flowed into gutters – but that was better than nothing. But now this older wiser and experienced man was speaking to him, speaking almost as a father to a son. And how he welcomed it. An older man speaking to him with the wisdom of experience and the guidance of a friend.

Our future director went home feeling much relieved. He strolled down to Gloucester Road underground with a spring in his step and bought his ticket, changed at South Kensington and took the Circle line, which was a nice long ride to King's Cross and lulled himself almost to sleep as he was rocked by the gentle rhythm of the train. At Embankment, a beautiful woman got on and sat almost opposite him and immediately buried her nose in her book. "I'd love a girlfriend like that," he thought. She looked like a pre-Raphaelite painting by Burne-Jones. She was wearing a close-fitting ankle length dress, which was so much the fashion then, and her hair was a Titian red. She wore little make-up but he noticed that her fingernails were painted shiny black. He tried not to stare but had to admit he was rather enchanted and was almost relieved when she departed. She lingered in his mind for several more stations but by the time he reached King's Cross she was only a vague and undisturbing memory.

The next day he came in with a couple of ideas to try on the class. He had been thinking about them for several days but had been blocked by indecision which seemed to freeze his ability to act on them but the school director's sympathetic words were like warm waves of care and understanding, and these waves penetrated deeply and the ice slowly melted away.

He entered the basement classroom and greeted the students who were all sitting around expectantly and somehow apprehensively. The young and future director took out a book. "We'll work on this," he said, "and I would like you all to buy a copy as soon as possible. We will make a play of it. Together. Slowly and patiently, and we will improvise some of it to create links between scenes." They all looked quite excited at the prospect of not having to do yet another play with only three or four good parts while the rest sat around and waited. "It's called *The Trial* by an author called Franz Kafka. Are any of you familiar with this work?" A few shot their hands up. "No matter, it's very easy to follow. So let's start. I'll read the first few lines and then we can act them out."

*"Somebody must have been lying about Joseph K. for without having done anything wrong, he was arrested one fine morning..."*

# 2.

# GOIN' BOWLING TONIGHT, EDDIE?

It was an understudy and ASM role, in other words, Assistant Stage Manager, which is how you start if your early beginnings were humble, that is if you didn't study at one of the first rate drama schools like RADA or Central. It meant your training was brief and exposure to audiences practically non-existent. However, like the other students you did get a chance on mass audition days to display your talents before a group of invited theatre directors and agents who were invited to comment on your carefully prepared effort and tear you to shreds if they felt so inclined. It was on one of those days towards the conclusion of his studies at a rather dingy drama school that was going through a period of severe decline, that he did his pieces. The academy was situated in the softer arboreal parts of Kensington and was only too glad to gather up the rejected applicants from the better and more famous institutions. Since the great names were heavily oversubscribed, the disappointed rejects were many and this humble academy managed rather by chance and not reputation to catch the odd bright spark. It was on the eventual reputations of these sparks who somehow managed to turn themselves into roaring flames that the school was able to catch some reflected glory.

It was a public audition for the industry and on the strength of his performance lay his chances of a future via an agent or being cast onto the dung heap ferreting for scraps. So he prepared carefully for the day when his test would come, when he would throw himself on the mercies of those professional viewers who were connected to that wide, profound and brilliant world of drama, of which he had not the slightest inkling, had not the slightest knowledge. It was a world he had brushed up against from time to time but only in the guise of an attendant sweeping the way before them. He had, in fact, once taken on a job as a salesman in one of the better menswear boutiques in Chelsea. It was the kind of job for those whose skills amount to just being able to communicate in the English language and to count to ten; be possessed of a certain amount of charm and an ability to woo your customer. That was all. The rest was comparatively simple if not mind-numbingly tedious except when it was busy.

The shop was run by a young man who one addressed as *Mr* John rather than the too familiar John. He was a very likeable fellow, pulled no rank whatsoever, was very approachable and so it was pleasant to work there. The only fly in the ointment was a rather dim-witted manager who liked to address the staff as if he was a sergeant major in the army. One day, the great and notorious Sir John Gielgud entered the shop, which to be fair was gaining a reputation for high-quality merchandise combined with innovative style, and the future actor served the famous player and even dared to ask of him how his current play was going and was answered politely and respectfully. Other notables of that profession came in and so he found himself on the edge of their world but no more able to penetrate it had there been a wall of glass between them.

But he loved these actors. They seemed to bring an aura of otherworldliness about them. They even had a kind of glow and while this may be pure imagination on the part of the future drama student he still felt that they were running on higher powered batteries. One day he was walking along the King's Road when he saw at a distance the absolutely unmistakable shape of Albert Finney walking towards him with a group of fellow actors. Of course, he had been rehearsing at the Royal Court, John Osborne's *Luther*. With his shorn head, Finney even resembled a German fanatical monk and conveyed such strength of purpose, such a clear focus in his stance that the salesman was totally captivated. He couldn't take his eyes off this young man only a couple of years older than himself and already triumphant and exuding the unmistakable aura of stardom. Finney entered the greasy spoon café, where everybody sat on long high-backed benches and ate roast beef and two veg followed by a pudding and custard, which nicely filled one up. Finney then went back to Lutherian explosions while this salesman returned to folding lambswool sweaters and stacking shirts.

So he did have a faint inkling of this world and hoped fervently that he would one future day open the door to that mysterious world. He had even worked in film as an extra, a valued and much in demand item since these were the days when the British film industry was thriving and extras were always needed. A friend had told him where to go; it was a small agency off Poland Street in Soho. He duly went, signed on, left two ten by eight glossy prints plus all the details of height, size etc. and then dutifully each evening, checked in for work as he was required.

The answer for the first weeks was invariably the monotonous repeat of the night before but one day it was "Report to Pinewood studio, stage five..." Oh! How damned, bloody, sodding exciting, he thought. So off he went by tube and then bus, reported at the crowd artists' office, was duly signed in, and sent to wardrobe for the crowd and got dressed as a cowboy, since his first movie was a Western.

Oh how wonderful, he thought, was this? How glorious, how divine was this, for now he was suddenly thrust, even as an extra, right into the middle of it and was sharing the scene with none other than the glorious, the sexy, the cute, Jayne Mansfield!! Then, after the first assistant gave the extras their action, which was basically just flopping around the set like grimy drunken cowboys, they were privileged to watch Miss Mansfield perform a burlesque song and being coached at the same time by the choreographer. This was a dream! He had entered this other world. He was in their world, their marvellous, brilliant, amazing, dazzling world and he was spellbound. Over and over they did it. The taped music started afresh and the brilliant male choreographer so cleverly impersonated all those sexy female gestures for her dance routine as if he were to the manner born, which she copied and got better and better at. This was showbiz with a capital S! Our young and future actor was spellbound. What a divinely lovely lady she was and so very determined to get it right. But in reality he was no more than a ghost to them and at the end of the day he picked up his lovely five pounds and went contentedly home.

He did this work for many months and among many great and famous artists, but now, now he was about to leave his sultry Kensington drama school having been a student and some might say, a zealous one. He performed his first piece, which was from a modern American play by William Saroyan and did it well since he knew it backwards having been his favourite party piece for some time. He followed it with a speech from Hamlet. His soliloquy was torn to shreds by a clever examiner but he was prepared for criticism and didn't take it badly at all. Later a list was pinned on the wall of all those who attended and one of them was an actor's agent. His name was John Penrose, a friendly, plump and cherubic agent who was once a reasonably well-known actor and was now an agent with an office in Cambridge Circus. The young actor-to-be phoned the agent the day after the audition and Penrose very charmingly said he was quite impressed by the actor's humble contribution and he was invited to his office for a meeting, which he attended the following day. He eyed the scripts piled to the ceiling and the smiling photos of his clients – it was so typical of an agent's office it might have been a stage set.

The agent said that while he admired the young man's energy and verve he thought he looked rather sour when receiving criticism from the director about his Hamlet speech.

Actually, the actor-to-be reassured him that he wasn't and was just as happy to be thrashed as be praised since he was at least being tested and judged and there is nothing more that an actor can ask for. Can one? Having reassured Mr Penrose that he was not about to join the bulging ranks of the temperamental, inebriated and psychotic actors that had been the fashion as of late, he added that he was a reasonable and highly dedicated chap who could be relied on. Thus reassured, the agent informed him that there was a tour going out of an Arthur Miller play called *A View from the Bridge* and there was a job as ASM and small part player. The name of the character was Louis. He was to stroll on and casually shout out the line (he had about three) "Goin' bowling tonight, Eddie?", hear the response and then saunter offstage. The rest was stage management, which he would share with a marvellously ebullient and charming Ozzie stage manager. It was an exciting first day and he took the bus from Chelsea where he had managed to rent a small room in a friend's flat. Got off at Piccadilly, walked up Windmill Street and climbed the stairs of the pub on the corner of Windmill and Brewer. Introduced himself and was sent straightaway to work and get some props which in this case was fruit from Berwick Street market since they needed some on the dinner table.

Apart from this he had to keep the 'book' which was the production prompt book. Now, there is a special way of marking all the moves in your prompt book so that the actors can ask you if they forget where they are supposed to be and you can respond in seconds. One writes the moves simply in the blank page opposite the script with a number and then circles the number by the actual word on the printed page. So cross down centre stage becomes (xdc) or cross up left becomes (xul). P is prompt side, which is where the prompter sits and is usually (dsl) in the corner under the pros arch. O.P. is opposite the prompt side and so on and so forth and so it is very useful to have done some stage management since it gives one a feeling of the mechanics of the stage and it's a good apprenticeship, especially if one is going to entertain the idea of being a *director*. Most of the young bloods leaving the top drama schools would never consider doing stage management, not even for their first job since they would think it implies a lowering of status, but it is true to say that the loss is theirs. Working with the director and writing down accurately the moves with sound cues and light (lx) gives one such a broad sense of the whole dynamics of the play and an appreciation of the actors who come to rely on you for their moves, words, props etc.

So he went to work with a will and greatly admired the quartet of actors who made up the family. They seemed to be so secure in their roles and so easy with the American accents that they might almost be making up the lines as they went along. He loved watching them and was amazed at how each time they rehearsed it was exactly as it was before without ever getting stale. The young girl lead always grabbed her chair by the kitchen table and heaved her knees under it, as she enthused about something, always, in exactly the same way and it was wonderful to observe. She was a pretty girl with sparkling energy and portrayed sheer innocence. The young boy playing Rodolpho was just brilliant and how proud he was to at last be part of it. This was real. He was in the theatre! He was happy!

It was now time for the first performance, which ironically was to be just down the road from his parents' home in Finsbury Park. It was a magnificent old barn called the 'Finsbury Park Empire'. The theatre was huge. It was a palace and more – it was a gigantic auditorium, a grand temple of the arts. And most of all it was frightening beyond belief. Yes, he would be going on that night and the thought of it seemed totally unreal and fear gripped his soul in its icy fingers. This was a baptism of fire beyond anything ever experienced in his entire life. He even dreaded that he would not be able to do it, not even be able to walk across that immense territory called 'the stage', and say his lines with any voice or conviction.

That night he performed all his stage management duties. He sat in the prompt corner and cued the sound when the red light flashed on. Then he walked across the back of the stage behind the backcloth to stand by for his entrance and his one line. He was dressed in the seaman's navy coat and woollen 'beany' hat. Eddie Carbone, the lead, was on the forestage which represented the 'street' scene. The actor's moment was coming up. His heart pounded. He even thought he might expire, die there on the spot. Eddie is on stage and has said the cue line for the actor to enter. But he can't. His legs feel frozen to the spot but then suddenly he feels himself start to move as if some mysterious force has come to rescue him, to save him from damnation. He is strolling on and it feels as if he is in a gigantic cavern that has no end. He had never been in such a space in his entire short life and so he crossed the stage not looking to his right, not daring to face that vast maw of emptiness.

He felt he was walking through purgatory and yet in the distance, he could see the lead actor just waiting, smiling at him. Yes, he is actually grinning at the nervous beginner as if he is pleased to see him and the actor fastened his eyes to him as if they were the only link he had that saved him plunging in to the infernal depths. The actor is now close to him and his smile has not left his face. His great craggy smile and now he is close to Eddie Carbone and what does the great man do? He throws one arm around his shoulders as if in greeting. He never did that in rehearsal. "My," he thought, "what a man, what guts, what fearlessness to care about me." To haul him over to the other side since he could see the fear, could feel his fear. He thought, "I love you mister," took a deep breath and said, "Goin' bowling tonight, Eddie?"

# 3.

# LINCOLN – A PROVINCIAL REP

The giant cathedral loomed up in the distance as the train steamed into Lincoln station and he never forgot that first image, the massive edifice of stone rising out of the town seemed to be a comforting symbol. He walked to the theatre, a smallish but charming old Victorian pile sitting on a prominent corner of the street. He entered the building and soon he was sitting opposite the director, a heavy set and rather matronly woman, however they had a good chatter and he read a piece of Orlando, the young hero in *As You Like It*. He must have impressed her somewhat since straightaway she implied that he would fit the role admirably, to which remark he was double-chuffed and thankful, grateful and happy, and conveyed all this in oodles of smiles and nods which were of course all meant. So happily he went back to the station with Orlando pinging around his brain and two weeks later he was up there with bags and baggage plus a nice Victorian beautifully made wooden make-up box, which had once been a tea container.

He also had quite decent digs in an old house on the higher slopes of Lincoln where several other actors also stayed. They were an amiable group and he immediately bonded with them. One of the actors had just played Billy in *Billy Liar* and was fond of telling him how the locals used to shout out if they passed him in the street, "Hello Billy!" And that seemed to have made him very proud, and why not. They went to a rehearsal room across the road from the theatre and all sat down for the first read through, which was just about the weirdest read through he had ever experienced, since every Shakespeare sexual innuendo was cut out even when it not only truncated the text but robbed it of all meaning. Every 'maids', 'meddlers', 'pricks', etc., etc. was surgically excised. After a while, he gently reminded her that this classic text had not been cut for decades, but the matron held her ground. However, further cuts resulted in a bit of banter between the two, which was watched with much smirking by the rest of the cast, who obviously knew her too well to engage in any debate.

At first the discussion was reasonably amicable, arguing for the text, for Shakespeare, for the poetry, the response of which was that this was going to be played to schools and some of the more suggestive bits would not be suitable for young people, but as the cuts came with greater and greater swiftness the discussion became acrimonious until in the end it became impossible to even address the intransigent lady. He wondered how on God's earth did such a woman ever get to run a theatre, especially if she couldn't bear what theatre sometimes does, and is meant to do, which is to mirror every aspect of the human soul in all its bizarre and multitudinous ways, with all its sores and blotches. Here was the censor, of all people, Shakespeare!

But the days passed and the cuts somehow healed up and he got on with the main goal of learning all those other lines and dealing with the scenes that remained in, and there were plenty of those. Each morning before rehearsal he had a session with the training master who was coaching him and another actor for the opening scene – a dynamic wrestling match into which he really threw himself, allowing his rival to get the better of him with some daring falls and throws to make Orlando's eventual conquest more dramatic. Since this was a school-touring production, visiting neighbouring towns like Rotherham and other godforsaken places, the set and costumes were fairly simple, if not ghastly. They would be bussed in and then after the show bussed out again. So this was the routine after an initial two-week run in the pretty but decaying old theatre. A very good actor was playing the saturnine philosopher Jaques, who looked good and spoke the lines well and Rosalind and her friend were played by two very charming ladies, except there was zero chemistry between them, which could just have well, he surmised, been his own fault. The Duke in exile was played by a prematurely balding and delightful actor called John who bonded with him almost immediately and was a font of charm and wit.

Although not in the play, there was an Irish actor in the company called Wesley, who he also befriended. He was charming and handsome and had a touching and almost unendurable lust for any female who crossed his path and when describing his conquest would almost salivate in his relish in describing the event. So the Irishman and he became good mates and were to remain mates for many years. Life was pleasant at the small theatre in Lincoln, and he even met and courted a lovely, if slightly hefty, local girl who was sweet and pretty, and so one might say that life was as complete as it could be for a young player away from home. Theatre does become your surrogate family for you have brothers, sisters, mothers, fathers and even wicked uncles as well as local lovers and a nice little home to take them to and no responsibility except to get on that stage sober every night and do your best. Theatre can be a healing experience as long as you give your best to it. Suddenly, the schoolgirls' fan letters came; they came like an avalanche, sweet, charming, passionate, enthusiastic and even well written. They claimed they admired him for his performance, his style, his courage, as displayed in the wrestling scene, and they all ended the same way with a heartfelt request for a signed photo. Never having had a response anything like this before, he had no photos to give, so he took one of his few larger ten by eight publicity shots to the local photo shop and had a couple of hundred small ones printed off and dutifully replied with the desired signed photo to all of them: to all of those sweet, childish, innocent, nubile females who became enchanted with a young male on stage expressing his love for Rosalind, and who hardly realised he had little to do with Rosalind, and for some reason barely connected with her – there wasn't an ounce of electricity between the pair of them. He did his daily tour to the dull and dreary towns and the director always accompanied them like a seething sergeant major and things were getting more and more strained for this weird one could not leave him be but kept giving him petty nit-picking notes until at the end he had to tell her to "Shut up!" This made him feel like a delinquent, a naughty, nasty kid spitting back at his ghastly but well-meaning teacher or his Mum.

Work had developed into a routine: during the day he would go into town and buy some steak and veg to cook up a delicious meal for lunch, then go to the theatre and clamber aboard the bus, sitting as far away from the director as possible. On his return he'd sometimes meet up with his beloved of the largish hips and luscious mouth and feast on her throughout the night.

One day, she sweetly asked him to have Sunday lunch with her family who were quite well-to-do and cultivated people since her father was a respected doctor. However, she had a most extraordinary and quite fascinating surname taken from the French, which unfortunately we are not at liberty to mention. So the actor, never really feeling at ease with cultivated, proper people, was doing his level best to be charming and pleasant and jovially discussed the joys of playing Shakespeare, when her father made one of those remarks, meant to be taken as a kind of compliment and yet can be so easily interpreted as a most terrible comment on the pathetic recipient on whom the remark is aimed. As the chatter got to the subject of the economy, he rather suddenly blurted out, "Look at poor Terry here, an actor, struggling on tuppence a week and does the poor man complain? No, he still gives it his all, don't you Terry?"

Suddenly all eyes looked to him at the table and he felt the blood rush to his face as if he had been given a hearty slap. He tried to smile and shrug it off but couldn't quite put the words together and fumbled lamentably, "Er, yes, well, but it's not really so bad." Of course the doctor was trying to pay the poor struggling and silent actor a compliment but since Terry's ego was a little like Humpty Dumpty the slightest adverse wind would send it crashing mightily to the ground. He felt as if he had been shot. He felt rooted to the chair and couldn't answer humorously in the spirit in which it was meant. He was a poor actor earning a pittance and suddenly, what he had been so proud of, now filled him with shame, especially in front of her father, this elegant, sophisticated doctor. That little comment just slipped out without a second thought and no malice was intended whatsoever but suddenly he felt weak and small, a pathetic actor in a tatty production, and just as he bathed himself in the virtues of his great and noble calling, he could equally plummet into the worst nagging doubts about the downside. Now in front of his inamorata, he felt shabby and couldn't wait to leave the table.

Nevertheless his spirits were restored as the tour came to a close. Gathering his huge batch of female fan letters into a pile he put them into a cardboard box intending to keep them forever-more. He wasn't asked to stay on for any more plays even though by now he had a massive fan base in the town and would have increased the box office considerably, but the poor old batty director had had enough of him. She continued in this position for some time after his departure until she ran out of audiences who were willing to endure the half-baked shows she inflicted on them and eventually the curtain fell for the last time.

However he did keep up his friendship with Wesley for some years and his Lincoln girlfriend came to London a few times but they soon real-ised they had little in common outside of that small town. The little environment of Lincoln somehow held them together as is often the case with repertory romances. He often wondered what had happened to her. Soon he had even forgot-ten he was ever there but was reminded of the event when walking down Islington High Street he came across the actor who played his wrestling opponent. He had opened a small antique shop in Islington. For some reason actors often end up going into antiques.

One significant thing came out of Lincoln. He was wandering inside the magnificent cathedral when he came across a plaque dedicated to the strange boy who features in the tale *Hugh of Lincoln*. It was claimed at the time that he had been murdered by the local Jews as a kind of ritual sacrifice. Of course, it was a set-up job to accuse the Jews, who were Lincoln's moneylenders, of the crime. In this way the debtors could easily rid themselves of their debts, which were considerable. It was a horrendous and tragic event, which led eventually to the Jews being turned out of England once they had been bled dry of their wealth, and therefore their use.

One day, Terry, being miserably out of work and feeling a little more worthless than usual, decided to try and write a play about that strange and macabre event in Lincoln eight centuries ago. For his research he joined the reading room of the British Museum and from the enormous amount of information available on Hugh of Lincoln wrote his first play. He called it *Hep! Hep! Hep!* an acrostic for 'Hisrolyem Est Perdita!' *Jerusalem is Lost*. It was the shout the crusaders used when with swords drawn they attacked the Jews and Saracens. Suddenly, he became a playwright, so Lincoln was the path that was necessary for him to take and he was even thankful to that small pretty theatre and having to stomp around the Forest of Arden in that soppy costume. There *was* a reason for it!

# 4.

# TAKE-OVER

He had actually seen the play and was mightily impressed so when his agent rang and told him that they were seeing people for some replacements when the play returned, he was over the moon. Having seen it already felt like a good omen, and although it was a minor role, the character was on stage for the duration. His vocal enthusiasm for the production may have tilted the eminent director's opinion favourably towards him. So, without more ado he was cast for the play's extension at one of London's most prestigious theatres!

He was one of a team of low-life, second-rate pastry chefs working in a gigantic kitchen in one of those huge hotels that were always on the go 24/7. No doubt the distinguished author saw in the kitchen an apt metaphor for the world with all its struggles and conflicts, and the cast themselves were indeed like a league of nations. It was a good team of actors and he got on with most except for a couple of cynical sods, which out of a company of nearly twenty was not too bad.

Some of the actors were a bit on the weak side but they all fitted in except for one pretty nasty piece of work whom he believed was a touch mental since she could not help making sour comments at every opportunity and so he avoided her sight and presence for the entire run. But the star was exceptional and made a gallant job of replacing the original actor who himself was nothing less than stupendous and he remembered how electrifying he was when watching it several weeks earlier, and much envied his skill and panache.

So one morning he made his way to the great theatre, which ironically was in the same street as a menswear shop he had worked in just a few years ago. In the same street, and now he got off at the same tube, Sloane Square, but to what a difference! This was his beginning. The director got stuck in, and speedily, since he was only replacing three or four actors in a very large cast. The new lead was very handsome and went at it with spirit but the director had a reputation for sarcasm and bitchiness and the new star's grace and good looks, let alone his privileged background, gave ample target for the director's acidic barbs but these were taken with a goodwill since the director was somewhat held in awe.

The actor's role was but a small link in the chain of events that goes towards the final result, the great culinary feast. He was on the extreme right side of the stage, which was his workstation, shared with an eccentric actor who was, he supposed his superior. This actor also played the part of a pastry chef. He was a comic cockney with a mighty anarchic streak, but they got on just fine since the newcomer was not unwilling to act as his apprentice.

The first rehearsals were in a large rehearsal room off the King's Road, Chelsea, and the director went at it with a will aided by a very sharp assistant. The writer was there each day watching the proceedings with a proud and proprietorial eye, lounging louchely back in his chair, his hair fashionably long since this was the beginning of the liberated Sixties, when even bank clerks at your local branch wore shoulder-length hair and young pretty girls wore skirts up to their knickers and every male walked around with a semi-permanent erection. Being a mixed bunch of actors; Irish, Jewish, Greek, English, of mainly working-class upbringing made for easy communication except for the sour lady, who was foul beyond the call of duty and the most bitter hag he had yet come across. He could never be bothered to try and interpret the cause of her hate since he had done absolutely nothing that might have offended her. Perhaps it was the 'time' when people had little restraint and were encouraged to let it all hang out so to speak, so he avoided her like the plague. Even the bona-fide working class author who just sat there day after day in his chair hardly addressed him.

Once he got going in his rather small role, he attacked it with as much resourcefulness as the small role could muster but the director paid perfunctory attention to him and saved his venom for the leading actor who bore it all with such dignity, it was a lesson to watch. Maybe he thought that this was his method of directing and should just submit himself for the onslaught – to break doors down, humiliate, jibe, insult and all done with a jokiness, so that's alright then. Like I'm the flavour of the month director and you're just an upper-class ponce from Eton. The young hand-some lead took it all in his stride and was splendid in the part. There was another actor (one of the two unpleasant ones) who was especially vile to the point where he would gladly have thumped the twerp but managed to avoid him for most of the rehearsal and the short run, as he had the other sour maiden. Most of the actresses were never heard of again although some of the male actors did have quite considerable success in the theatre world including the lead who, with his handsome looks, charm and beautiful voice, hardly stopped working, until his rather sad and premature demise in later years. This talented man was sensitive to a fault and had become more so over time and possibly this had contributed to his gradual isolation and death.

There was always much talk of the production transferring to the West End but sadly, it was not to happen. Perhaps the cast was too large and therefore expensive but it was a very powerful play marred only by the odd lapse when the kitchen staff, between shifts, began melancholically philosophising. The climax came when a fight broke out towards the end of the play, followed by the angry entrance of the restaurant owner. This dignified Greek came on stage and made a very powerful speech which was the crux of the play, centred around why can't there be peace in the world blah, blah... However, it held the audience spellbound and came at just the right time.

In his role as a pastry cook he had a bowl and whisk but no ingredients, since these were all mimed which appealed to him enormously. He was told to make a cake from the very beginning, starting with the eggs, which he mimed breaking into the bowl and whisked them with the flour to make the pastry and sometimes he would delicately scoop some fragments of eggshell that might have slipped in. He was involved in some spirited group action but always returned to his little space in the corner. His charming partner, Harry, had the strange habit of pushing his station further and further offstage but the young actor would fiercely hold onto his territory and assume that this is what greedy ambitious actors do to each other and it never angered him. Sometimes the play would erupt with humour and the audience laughed at some piece of business and at such times his partner would whisper, "Kill it … kill it," in other words, suppress the laugh that was so painstakingly striven for. He obeyed him by engaging in a sudden whirlwind of whisking which inevitably drew the audience's attention away from the laugh. This was a thoroughly shameful thing to do. His partner was not malevolent, more a cockney harlequin who couldn't help making mischief.

Standing outside the pub after the show one summer night he realised, when he heard Harry talking politics with the Assistant Director, what a brilliant analytical mind he had and just how astoundingly ignorant in comparison he felt he was. The young actor was hearing for the first time the new energy of the Left and how engaged the followers were and how very informed. These were the heady days of Cuba, Dubček, Tito, the Berlin Wall, the Hungarian uprising, and these people were on the pulse while the rest of the ignoramuses could only talk about 'Swinging' London, dope and mini skirts.

The play was most successful on its re-run and they all went to the pub next door after the show which was your typical English seedy, run down, funky pub with a pinball machine in the corner. At that time the theatre was building up its reputation as a writers' theatre, attempting to discover radical writers of the new age but it was really a directors' theatre, and so a few of the 'elite' would gather in the pub and play the pinball machine. Being an uncouth, raw, uninformed but idealistic youth he tended to overrate these directors and see them as demi-gods with special access to arcane sources of knowledge, but something about them also stuck in his craw. He didn't find them a particularly pleasant bunch and he was glad when it was all over.

There was a lovely Jewish casting woman who was obviously terribly glad to be in the wolf's lair and so walked around with a hangdog face. Thinking no doubt that this was appropriate for a dangerous revolutionary cell, and naturally hoped that her expression would at least prevent her from being found out.

The director was quite friendly and seldom if ever gave him a sample of his acid tongue, which really was more amusing than toxic and most of the actors liked him. He eventually went on to direct opera where he would meet divas much like himself. He worked like a demon and eventually dropped dead from exhaustion. In those early days the actor supported the Royal Court quite a lot since it was the most dynamic theatre in London and the plays they put on were dangerous, exciting and mostly foreign. The theatre was one of the few places where one could see Brecht, Sartre and Max Frisch. Also the theatre employed really bravura actors. He recalled the first time he went there one afternoon to see Christopher Logue's *The Lily White Boys*, directed by Lindsey Anderson with Albert Finney when he was a young, handsome, thick-haired real piece of Britain. There was no one like him then. Oh well, that was in its heyday.

# 5.

# A CRAP JOB

Sometime ago he was actually offered a job, yes an acting job in quite a well-known provincial theatre famed for performing classics. It was also known as a training ground for young, still spotty-faced directors, freshly graduated and terribly keen to leave their spoor on some notable terrain. He was cast in *The Merchant of Venice* as one of those subsidiary roles that Shakespeare's plays are littered with and that few in the audience ever remember. However his agent, perhaps still unaware of the potential of his new young client, had him down for the 'C' group. Yet despite his low ranking in the play, the young actor ended up coaching one of the poor sods who had a part that he could have played on his head. Never mind, he had a job, and even if it was a total waste of time, energy and effort as well as being dispiriting, it was a good mark on his CV to have worked there. He was *working*, a verb so vitally important in a poor actor's life. It may not be what he had trained so assiduously hard for, had read hundreds of plays for, had thrown himself wholeheartedly into the turbulent theories and systems of Antonin Artaud, Stanislavski, Bertolt Brecht. Had argued in coffee-houses, lips trembling with cappuccino froth as he spat out some ill-digested theories of Expressionist theatre and feeling like a revolutionary while rolling a line of Samson's Dutch tobacco, but it was work.

So while he strutted, puked, posed and dreamed, he always saw himself as an acting titan and rushed to see the great Olivier on stage and then left the theatre so infected by the sheer charisma of the man that he even ended up talking like him for several days. Of course, actors in their cups, and frequently unemployed, would gather in the once famous thespian pub, The Salisbury, situated in theatreland, and would need little prodding to find an opportunity to do their 'Brando', 'Bogart' or 'Olivier' as if they were burping up bits of them that had lodged in their gullet. And these mini 'perfs' would somehow indicate that they were really rather splendid actors. In fact, they were poor dogs feeding on the shadows of their heroes, the giants that they could never be, except perhaps for a few seconds in the pub.

So to get back to our young keen actor travelling on a train to Pissville, an area of no particular interest in what is drearily called the Midlands of Britain, an area of sheer unadulterated horror, whose prime virtue seems to be that nobody feels challenged. Nobody feels excited enough to do anything with their lives except live until the clock stops and hope that nothing untoward will happen to them to shake them into a higher mode of consciousness. No, just to be content to amble on, watch TV, a trip to the Costa Brava once every two years for a touch of the nearly exotic although most of their hotels on that hellish strip are even more ruthlessly British than those in Britain.

However, in nearly every one of those ghastly Midland towns you will find a theatre, a live theatre, which gives the town a little cultural status. It's usually a relic of the time when 'live' theatre was a stirring event when some great and even legendary actor would tread their boards during a lengthy trip from the capital. Sometimes the great ones would undertake this as a 'try-out' before a West End run.

Leading actors acquired a reputation akin to stalwart gladiators taking on a half dozen leading roles in as many days and then trudging onto the next gig, leaving the townsfolk eagerly chatting about the great man's visit for years to come. In times long gone the stars were spared the chore of touring with a company, let alone the vast expense, since the 'local' team would be familiar with the most popular Shakespeare plays. So illustrious were some of the actors that years later plaques were inscribed with details of the event and proudly hung on the theatre walls. The theatres thrived and the locals were virtually hanging from the rafters. Then a change took place: stage managers became the directors. In the early days when directors like Tyrone Guthrie and Joan Littlewood formed strong partnerships with actors, the theatres were still hothouses for some exotic blooms. Later theatre became 'respectable' enough for university students and it was thought that a smart academic mind would be more useful, someone who can 'analyse' the text and explain to the dumb humble actors what line endings, scanning rhythms and iambic pentameters were. The actors sat and listened with mouths half open and sore arses from hours of sitting where once they would be up and doing the effing thing.

And so with his case packed and make-up box replenished – the actor's favourite, the Victorian tea box, he checked in at the theatre, was allocated some rather spartan digs and made his way to the theatre the very next morning for a read through.

The prior night was spent meeting all the newcomers in the bar who were getting quietly sozzled, and exchanging boring tales usually to do with friends they had in common and plays recently seen and loved or loathed and performances belittled, but this clucking and mooing was more to do with establishing their status.

Freshly shaved and feeling somewhat keen and jaunty, he entered the large foyer where the actors were gathering, meeting and greeting the regular company who had been playing the night before. There were yelps of recognition and enthusiastic hugs as actors met up with old colleagues from previous encounters and then much chatter would be devoted to "How was so and so?" and when they had run out of all they had in common they would return to their chairs and idly flip through their scripts. Among the newer fraternity mostly brought in to swell the ranks, the chatter seemed to centre largely on what Indian or Chinese caffs had won their approval, since a bunch of them went out the night before after the boozy session in the bar. He felt a little put out having not only missed the event but had spent a miserable night alone in his digs with a takeaway since he didn't wish to sit around mindlessly drinking and saw that his sobriety had caused him pangs of loneliness. He made up his mind to engage with them more.

Now the director came in clutching his script, which had been neatly bound into a large folder. He had an air of great confidence and assurance. For a few moments he stood by his chair in the centre of the semicircle of chairs that had been laid out and said in bright clear tones how much he welcomed the newcomers and hoped it would not be long before they got the hang of the place and what a friendly town it was and how much they supported the theatre and now, we'll just have a read through of this fascinating and controversial play. And so they did. Though this actor's role wasn't large it did keep popping up and he had a nice little speech near the end. However, when he first read the play he tended to skip swiftly through until he found where he came to life once more, where once again the playwright had seen fit to raise him from the shadows. But now watching and hearing the other actors pace through their roles it seemed to take forever before his few lines surfaced and when they did, they were swiftly swallowed up by the advancing avalanche of actors.

When the principals spoke their roles, the director leaned forward, listened intently, smiled, while the other regular actors in the company chortled at some rather arch, gamey interpretation of the lines, never mind, he did have one nice speech at the end. Yes, he'll make some impression ... you'll see … but when he did come to that moment, he actually witnessed the director flicking through the pages and making notes! Eyes front!! No matter, the actor expanded his chest and gave the speech a lot of 'welly', as it is called by the acting fraternity, although he had no idea why.

Then the read through was over, and everybody smiled and broke into a chatter of approval. The general consensus was that this was a good dramatic play, well read, superbly cast when in fact the second half was the biggest piece of hogwash he had ever heard, nevertheless it was frequently done.

Now all the regular actors were leaning over each other cracking little jokes and lighting up fags. The director, having allowed this little respite for a fag and piss, called for attention. He praised all the actors for a good reading and how it lasted 2 hours 15 minutes, which rather surprised the actor since it felt like an eternity if not the whole blithering morning. "So," the director said. "We'll take a quick lunch break," and one arch voice camply droned out, "Oh please, not too quick darling" to no one in particular. So he went out and grabbed a sandwich in the bar, which was quickly devoured and then rolled a fag to smoke outside in the balmy spring sunshine. As he sucked the smoke into his lungs he thought that *it* was the best feeling he had had all morning.

He was about to return, when he spotted a very attractive woman who seemed to be in her late twenties or early thirties. She was drinking coffee at the far end of the bar, and he realised she had been eyeing him up. He caught her eye and in more of a reflex action gave her a hint of a smile. She actually responded in that slightly coy way as if she had been found out. And then he went into the foyer thinking strongly about her and how her presence was the only thing that had lit up his day.

So now they were back with the nice smiling director who began his dissertation on the play, as if he was sitting an oral exam for an honours degree. He talked. He talked first about the history, the history of Venice because the play takes place there and the complexity of its economics since the early Church forbade moneylending and how only the perfidious Jews were allowed to indulge in such a dirty trade, and then he discussed the comparative lending rates between various countries, and then he moved on to the source of the play and English history at the time and suddenly he went back to the thirteenth century since that was the last time that Jews were allowed in England, and then he droned on about how Shylock was really taking revenge for the past iniquities the Jews had suffered in England.

The actor was starting to wonder how he should do his last speech, and how he would give it style, give it some impact and suddenly his mind that had been taking it all in unhooked itself and focused on the smile of that very attractive and sexy lady who he hoped he would see again and so for a few moments he drifted happily on the seas of his own imagination.

Suddenly he heard some laughter and realised that the director had obviously made a joke and so the actor smiled just to show that he hadn't been dallying in little rock pools along the shore whilst the director was boldly sailing through oceans of verse. The director was talking about how important the verse was since it held the metre and the meaning of the play, and how one should respect the verse. Although the actor thought he had hardly any verse in the small role and in fact much of the play was not in verse, this idea or theme seemed to captivate the director who now got into stresses and beats and metre. The actor started to drift off again, but had to resist sleep and concentrated instead on the actors, some of whom were actually taking notes or smiling and nodding fawningly, and then he drifted off in a kind of semi-focused way that looked as if he was thoughtfully taking it all in.

He was thinking of that delicious squeeze in London who had been so kind to his priapic beast lately and whether or not he should invite her up. Why not? Maybe he'd invite her when the play was on but then might he feel a little uncomfortable about her seeing him in such a small role. "Who gives a monkeys," he thought, "it's work, and we can't always be heroes, anyway he desperately needed company." Just then the blonde in the coffee shop floated in front of his eyes, her smile was really sweet, yes, but that's a long shot, whereas his nice little squeeze was a sure-fire thing and she'd be so happy if he called her. Maybe just for a night, or maybe two, max.

He surreptitiously checked his watch. Christ it was 4 p.m., surely they're going to break so the evening actors could have a rest before the show and then this hell would be over and it was just as his mind was snapping on some juicy morsels of freedom, when the director slammed his book shut. The afternoon had slowly crawled by, weighted down by the solemn drone of the young director's erudition and the atmosphere was so heavy the minute hand of the clock could barely crawl up its face. At last, at last the clock hand moved to the appointed spot and thank God it was over. The director smiled, thanked all for their attention and actually apologised for finishing early to give the performing actors a bit of a break! For the last two hours the sheer monotony of the director's thin, cultivated voice had sent him wandering into his own dreamy world. Now the actors shot off with some pace as if justified by the need to prepare themselves for the night's performance, which nicely camouflaged their passion to get the hell out of that madhouse.

He drew some satisfaction towards the end of the 'lecture' when he saw some of the principals trying to suppress yawns and slouching in their chairs, the shape of their bodies revealed the state of their minds. He wasn't sure how long he could endure this, especially if this prat of a director was to continue in this vein the following day; sitting and listening while his limbs started locking and his muscles stiffened. And now yet another evening to pass, to while away, to kill, to sit in the bar drinking till some of the group decide to go out for an 'Indian' or a 'Chinese'.

He strolled into the bar and sucked in the fresh air from the open door, rolled a fag and ordered a coffee, but she was nowhere to be seen. Then he was joined by one of the small-part actors called George who seemed happy and smiling at everything and who eventually said, "She's a dishy lady, isn't she?" "Who?" "Oh, Who? The one you were staring at before, during the break." "My god, I didn't think it was so obvious." "It wasn't, not really, since I was clocking her too; she's the wife of the artistic director!" "God! Really!" "Yes, she is and a very nice lady … not the wife of the visiting director who's been boring the arse off us all day, but the overall director … John." "Oh, I see." "Yes, fancy a drink?" "Oh, maybe I'll join you later." George wandered off in the direction where a small group of actors were already imbibing the pints. Maybe tonight he would see the current play and that would pass the time well.

Not to seem aloof he went into the bar and ordered his first drink of the evening and while it was being poured looked casually around, and there she was at the end of the bar, talking to one of the leading actors and while she was talking, as if she had second sense, which it is believed many women have when sniffing testosterone in the air, she briefly looked up, just briefly and gave him the hint of a smile without for a second halting her flow of chatter to her companion. Oh, how that look galvanised him, how the pert slinky hint of a smile from a strange woman sent a thousand pictures through the brain. He smiled, almost hesitantly back.

Of course, she was merely being ambassadorial on behalf of her husband and giving a touch of warmth from the hostess. That was all. Yes, that was all. And then his mind went back to seeing the evening show since his new mate George was determined to see it so he might as well and 'bond' a bit at the same time. Something to do and so they did and actually it wasn't half bad, and the play's star was the same young man who was cast as Shylock in *The Merchant of Venice*, even if he seemed rather too young for the role. However, one could see that he was an accomplished actor and might, he thought, even be a tad younger than himself. "Never mind, never mind," he ruminated, "my time will surely come." He sat through the entire play, had a drink outside since the weather was still pleasantly warm, took home some Chinese takeaway and then fell into a fitful sweaty sleep.

The next day, he took a power walk to the theatre so he'd be ready and alert for what was hoped would be the first day of 'plotting', the first day of using one's voice and body, trying things out but shortly after he arrived the director said, "Look chaps, we're just going to work all the principal scenes first, so go away, learn your lines and we'll see you all first thing in the morning, OK?"

This somewhat shocked him since now, this was, he mentally whined, day three, including the travelling up, that he had wanked around the pisshole with this ever so charming young director, aka: ponce! He swiftly strode out, rolled a fag and puffed vigorously, then stepped back into the theatre bar, where some of the other actors were sitting and checking the daily papers for the movies. "What a waste of an actor's life," he thought, "what a pathetic sad waste," and compared, as he always did, his lot with that of a dancer who would be obliged to work out with the company daily, feel part of it and have a respect for his art, since they were the heart of the company but not these bums. But while bewailing his lot he glanced up and there she was again, like an apparition, the beautiful blonde lady with whom he had already shared two delicious smiles. She was sitting at one of the back tables with her coffee and the *Guardian* which she seemed to be reading quite intently. He became slightly perplexed, as one does when there is something one wishes to do more than anything in the world without quite having the courage to do it. Should he simply say something? Should he walk by? So he bought a coffee and decided that he would walk past her table feigning coolness, and just as he was doing this, just as he had his eye on a further table as if to demonstrate his total indifference to her presence, she looked up and said, "Good morning." She smiled directly at him. "How are you enjoying this lovely town of ours?" As he was searching for an appropriate answer she invited him to sit, "Unless you're rushing off?" "No,

actually we've just been released to learn our lines."
"Yes, on matinée days the directors work with the
principal actors, since they only have them for a
short time." "Of course, and quite understandable."
"So, you're not too busy?" her eyes now engaged
with his. She held the paper out to him. "There's
a super review in the *Guardian*," and set it down
in front of him. "I saw the play last night," he said,
"yes it was very good." And as he read the paper
that she held out for him he felt her little finger
just graze his, oh ever so slightly, and he even felt
her feminine warmth coursing through it and
though they were actually touching fingers she
didn't withdraw hers.

She had been married to the company director
for ten years and they had two children and she
passed all this information on to him quite casually and comfortably as if it was the most natural
thing in the world. She seemed even glad to tell
him the details of her life in such a matter of fact
way and he allowed himself just to swim in her
aura and bathe in her sweetness as if he had just
climbed out of a filthy cesspit. Her husband was in
London for the day to audition some actors for the
next season. He looked at her as she spoke and she
looked at him and as her voice was speaking her
eyes were also speaking, albeit in a slightly differ-

ent subtext. And as he was listening and taking in everything that she said, his eyes were responding.

That same afternoon he was deep inside her and the happiest he had been in years and what an extraordinary woman she was, just about everything a man could wish for and he fell immediately in love with her. "I don't need to ask you to be discreet do I?" He smiled. "I can see that you would be." "I'll take our secret with me to the grave," he gallantly responded. She smiled. He was pleased that she detected something in him that lifted him above the common hoard of actors. That day he somehow floated above the vile metropolis, above the dreary supermarkets and pubs, above the Burger King and Kentucky Fried Chicken and stayed happily in his own world.

The next day he prepared himself for the blocking and had indeed spent the previous evening going over and learning his lines. He walked into the rehearsal room and noticed that the chairs were still in the same semicircle as they were on the first day. The 'nice' director chirped brightly in, "We're all going to go through the play scene by scene and make sure that we're all on the same page." He hated that expression, so smart, so cool. And the director went through each scene telling the cast what it really meant and what the subplot was, and on and on he droned, and smiled at his own witticisms and occasionally the leading actors would make a suggestion or ask a question and so he'd go on and the day slowly groaned by. He thought only of her, of how beautiful and loving she was and what a gift had flowed into his arms. Oh yes, what an unforgettable, special gift.

That night he lay in bed, barely sleeping and waiting for the day to bloody dawn and when it did he made himself a cup of tea with his electric tea maker provided by the landlady and the actor felt that tea had never tasted so good. After draining the last drop, he simply packed his bags and left and as he hit the street the air never felt so fresh, freedom never tasted so clean. The morning was a bright clear blue one on which he would write the first deeds of the day ... escape! On the train back, he felt the strong rhythms of the engine surging through him as the countryside raced so innocently past. Of course he would miss her and had debated with himself what the consequences might be but eventually decided that escape was even more powerful.

# 6.

# A REMOTE REP COMPANY

*T*here've been a few gigs like that ... when the agent calls and asks, "Would you fancy going to Dundee for a few weeks?" or Barrow-in-Furness, or Chesterfield, or Buxton, or Rotherham, or Lincoln, or Perth, or Cardiff, or Coventry, or Nottingham, or Liverpool, or Edinburgh, or Glasgow, or Bromley, or Cambridge, or Cheltenham, or Palmers Green, or Newcastle, or even Greenwich which is nice and close. And that's where I went ... to every one of them and more. And in each one there was a special memory, an event, a performance, a person who affected you, who managed to etch into your memory something profound, and more than once your mind drifts back to them and wonders whatever happened to so and so, after you were so close, so intimate, so *friendly, like you might be mates forever and a day, and after you exchanged phone numbers swore that you would always keep in touch, that you would never let each other go, that you loved each other, needed each other and even lived for each other. Each person's company was a warm sustaining bath, since actors are like the walking wounded, preparing to face a different audience each night, rain or shine, in health or sickness and so much wanting to give of their best ... to be loved ... to get on that stage each night, confident or fearful, mad or sane. You could not just take a night off because you didn't feel up to it ... you had to do it ... you were a soldier of the theatre and that's what you did and your mates helped you through it as you did them.*

One day he auditioned for a little theatre in Perth, Scotland for their summer season. He took the long train journey from King's Cross and gazed in wonder as the landscape developed into that tawny Scottish look, that rugged, mountainous, dramatic scenery and he was stunned at the beauty of it all. "How lucky actors are," he thought, "since we are taken suddenly on these amazing journeys just to pursue our art. Yes, we are indeed a fortunate breed."

When he arrived at Perth station he hungrily inhaled that wonderfully pure mountain air and felt assured that all would be well in this glorious country of Scotland, since how could it not be when people spoke with such an innocent musical cadence that even their accent reassured him of their honesty and integrity. He took a cab to the theatre and was warmly welcomed and introduced to all the actors. He befriended two rather pretty and spirited English girls and two amiable blokes; the rest just seemed to fade into the background or just disappeared into an area of the brain filed away and marked 'no further interest'. It seemed strange for even though those actors were to work with him and rehearse with him, as soon as he left that theatre and that town he forgot they ever existed. But that is the nature of the strolling player who no sooner has left one theatre then is soon immersing himself in the lives of his next family of players. The first play in which he was cast was *The Importance of Being Earnest*, Oscar Wilde's delightful exposé of Victorian hypocrisy.

Now this was a bit of a stiff old production, directed by a rather astute middle-aged woman who seemed quite efficient, if a touch unyielding, but at least she got on with it and blocked it swiftly. He quickly entered into the spirit of the play and learned the lines and even added some moments of comic business but he couldn't deny to himself that he wasn't ideal casting even though he really had a go. Now he hadn't as yet found his actor's

'voice', his timbre and most of all his confidence…
all these were indeed growing and the more he
did the more they grew but like all artistic abilities
they needed time and there had not yet been quite
time enough. The result was that he was more than
often shit scared and faced the opening night with
some degree of trepidation but amazingly did get
through and the audience laughed at his antics and
he acquitted himself each night. His acting partner seemed equally nervous since Wilde is rather
precise, sharp and demands the best of an actor, in
fact it's as demanding as a piece of classical music,
like a Chopin Étude. So while both of the leading young men were nervous young neophytes,
together they managed to negotiate the evening
with few mishaps, as did the girls who seemed to
sail through as if their roles were written for them.

He was lined up for a series of plays since in
rep the director plans the entire season around the
actors that have been cast. It was fairly obvious
having worked with his present male acting partner,
that this chap was in no way as suitable for the role
of Stanley in Tennessee Williams' masterwork, *A
Streetcar Named Desire* still some weeks ahead, so
he assumed that role was to be his. However, the
next play was an E. M. Forster adaptation which by
happy chance he had seen in the West End only a
few weeks before and was, he thought, tailor-made

for it. The role was that of a likeable, virile, working-class Italian.

The one or two reviews for *The Importance* duly came out in the local papers and, while slightly critical of his performance, appreciated his humour and energy. The critic did suggest though that perhaps the casting was not ideal. It was a review he could live with but when the castlist was put up on the notice board for the next play, he saw to his bitter shame that he seemed to have been downgraded and that his fellow actor had been promoted and was cast as the fiery Italian which, he thought, was as wrong for that actor as it was right for him. Wrong, wrong, wrong, and unfortunately there is a certain age in which young men – and women for that part – cannot for a second project into the future, but must be satisfied now, absolutely now, as if the future does not exist, which in a way it doesn't except for those more phlegmatic and mature souls who seem to live more for the future than the present, and in this way all present disappointments are somewhat mitigated.

But he was not one of them. And living and thinking like that put the kybosh on any future plans he had for that charming little theatre in that charming but ever so slightly boring town of Perth. It's a pity that our actor did not at least have one smidgeon of wisdom to bite on the bullet of his disappointment and wait for the big one to come along which would then convince everybody including himself of his 'blazing' talent. But sadly this stoicism he had not yet developed, and therefore never learned to cunningly change adversity into opportunity. He was, one might say a touch 'feminine' in his inability to suppress, control or filter his emotions through plain common sense. Rejection and demotion was something he had had to deal with all his growing life and consequently was at an age when he was taking revenge for all the past slights.

By one of those strange coincidences a chap who had just been recruited to direct the play in which he had been demoted happened to be a friend he knew from London. While not wishing to harp on about the young actor's immaturity, this was also a time when friendships weren't forged from common interests so much as a desperation to have someone to talk to even if that person could not have been worse either in the role of supporter or ally.

This particular person had a grand eccentricity of laughing out loud in public with a stentorian bark which the actor found deeply embarrassing but put up with it. The laugh seemed to demonstrate 'oh just how bloody funny' he thought the whole thing was and how jovial, humorous and totally uninhibited he was. So behold out of all the reps in England who should be coming up but this charming, laughing hyena!!

Regrettably, not only was he of absolutely no comfort, he even became an alien and somewhat hostile presence, probably more concerned in securing his own future there than appearing to sympathise with the local rebel. Even then it's strange how a simple gesture can hook itself into one's mind forever more. It was possibly a Sunday evening and all the actors were sitting in the bar sipping gently on half pints when this director came in. With eagerness our young actor had been waiting for him and was brightened by his visit feeling that he might at least have an ally. As he entered the large room the actor indicated a space next to him at the table. The director, wishing to show just how 'sociable' he was, looked at the vacant seat proffered by his friend, smiled broadly and said, "I think I'll just sit over here," with much flourish as he sat among the other actors. He remembered flushing at the time and feeling really humiliated, it was a stupid and tasteless gesture and any warm milk of human kindness turned immediately to acid.

So straightaway with no advice from anyone, with no counselling from anyone who might have been able to shift the gears somewhat, since he had no one to ask except his own tormented over-sensitive alter-ego, he marched straight to the office of the pleasant elderly couple who ran the theatre, the long-established and respected theatre of Perth.

He gave his notice saying that he had rarely felt so unjustly treated. He told them that they had made a shocking mistake in not casting him as the fiery young Italian and giving it instead to this cool young Englishman actor who although reasonably efficient was totally miscast for the role. "I'm giving my notice and shall leave when the play closes." They both protested that not only was this unethical but illegal since he had signed up for the whole season and would get into great trouble if he took that action. With that threat the young actor's hackles rose and he even threatened to leave before the run of the play, that he would do a walkout there and then if they threatened him further.

Who knows from whence such outburst sprung. The poor confused management of course would have had no idea of the past disappointments the actor had had to deal with, or perhaps of the betrayals much further back in his murky past that stuck much deeper in this actor's craw, or those wounds in his system had never really healed. Betrayal was something that he was not prepared to stomach ever again. Of course, the giant shadow of his father loomed over much of his life until one day he would certainly dispel it. Although it is true to say that one never really manages to banish it forever.

Also he had felt very isolated since he started there a few weeks earlier and was bitterly lonely in his digs where no other actors were housed and had to sit with well meaning but simple working men with whom he had little in common except a draining sense of remoteness. He eventually changed his digs when a room in another actor's house became available and at least there was some company. There was one bright day however, before the play opened, when the set was being put up and he actually suggested that they all go visit Pitlochry where he had a young actor friend. And as one of the cast could drive they rented a car and drove to Pitlochry. It was a lovely drive and they had afternoon tea with his friend who was most charming and welcoming and just a whisper superior since Pitlochry was considered one of Scotland's best theatres, and they had a summer festival to boot!

Nevertheless the loneliness, combined with the chilliness of the company and then the betrayal of the role for which he had been earmarked was all too much to take and he left on the last night as he had promised. Of course, he certainly would not have left before the run as he had threatened.

He never heard from, or about any of those charming young actors from Perth rep ever again and of course he had no doubt that the pleasant, venerable couple who ran the theatre must have spent many hours over the years telling the story of that horrible, temperamental and selfish actor. Now as fate will sometimes have it, just a few months after leaving that pleasant and uneventful town he landed the part of a lifetime – highly demanding role but one that this time might have been expressly written for him. And lo and behold, he won blazing reviews in nearly every newspaper in London! He seldom thought of those actors in that little rep again ... although he never quite forgot them and even in some way was grateful to them, after all. Without them ...

# 7.

# TITUS!

O h this was to be the big one, an epic, revolutionary production of Shakespeare's goriest blood-fest and he was cast as one of the many sons of the tragic hero Titus Andronicus and whilst there wasn't really much meat on the bone he thought, "I can do something with it. Yes, make something of it." Is this not what all hopeful actors try to do? Compensate for the size of the role by dextrous handling of the text and induce the sun to shine on them for just a few moments. There is always that time in the play when your character must enter the spotlight of the audience's attention and for a few precious moments you become the vital link in the play, when all eyes are on you, holding on to the other links, one in each hand.

So, all the actors met at the friendly young director's flat and he addressed all of them and dazzled them with his erudition, his wit, his savvy, and talked brave, bold words about how he 'saw' the play as he had already produced the play for the Edinburgh Festival where it achieved a bit of notoriety. On the strength of that he was bringing it to London, to one of the great, rough theatres called the Roundhouse in Chalk Farm.

This was a theatre that embraced 'the radicals', 'the outsiders' the lunatic fringe who would find few welcoming theatres elsewhere. The Roundhouse was still raw, still being baptised by wild legions from the underbelly of other societies in other nations. It was a place favoured by the *cognoscenti*. As soon as he entered that great building he felt that without any doubt that this is where he belonged. And he did belong. This was his home, his sanctuary, his temple where he lay down his sacrificial offerings.

So the young director spoke and spoke and inspired dreams of glory, dynamic excitement, linguistic pyrotechnics à la Antonin Artaud, whose very name coruscated through excitable brains and this new cast went home thoroughly happy, ready to be stretched on the rack of great drama until the bourgeois fat popped out of our soft Chekhovian loving bodies.

The next day all the actors dutifully and eagerly turned up to rehearse at the Roundhouse in an area upstairs where they had reserved a place for them. But the rehearsals were not full of the whiff of cordite and the shocks of thunder that were promised in the young director's opening oration. They were just, normal, ordinary, even a tad uninspired but maybe he was what they call blocking it, to give the actors the shape, like an architect laying out the area before the magnificent structure goes up. Perhaps later our brains, hearts, and viscera would be churning and our livers smoking. And so he calmed his growing doubts. He told himself to be patient for now and go along with it, and he shouted out his lines with not too much relish since they seemed to come out of nowhere, in other words not given a context in which they might thrive. Lines without purpose or direction are like seeds thrown on the sand.

The days slowly and uneventfully passed, and slowly but surely the canker was creeping into his body, for something did not gel. Earlier when the nice young Oxbridge director had made his speech to the troops at the opening gathering, there was talk of speech patterns, dynamic physicality, the offering of the great God Artaud whose name must be whispered, whose life was hallowed; you draw in your breath when you even dare to mention the theatre God. This man whose name alone could summon up goblins and succubae, and so each day he patiently waited for just the beginning of the ritual that was promised and yet for whatever reason it was not forthcoming.

Spiritual hunger was beginning to leech goodwill from his once so enthusiastic bones and one morning when the director just said, "Oh, here you come on from stage right," he suddenly exploded, "Why!! Bloody Hell, why?" "Where have I been and what have I been doing? What shocking traumas have I been through with my beloved sister, who has been virtually undone, unseamed, raped, mutilated?" The director could only stare at him, frozen by the blast of his assault, the actor continued, "Just come on from stage right?" The poor actress who was full of goodwill obediently entered ready to do her 'shtick' but it felt so miserably empty, so shallow, forlorn and so this vehicle, this machine of blood and muscle called an actor just could not move. The actor said, "Forgive me but I cannot do this. I just don't know, I have no idea on earth what I am doing." And at that moment he decided to leave and only when he left that building, that temple that had seen the results of his own theatrical birth did he feel the spirit slowly returning to him refilling his veins. Suddenly stepping out of that stale rehearsal room made him feel pure, cleansed, he felt as if he had ripped some loathsome beast out of his guts. Ah! The smoky, gritty, dusty air of Camden smelt as pure as a field of roses and Antonin Artaud sang in his heart and he heard the reverberations of the great insane old master and then knew what he had to do and so went home and sat at the beautiful strong wooden desk that his good friend Alistair had made, yes, the very same man who built the 'execution bed' in *The Penal Colony*. The actor was so proud of his desk and felt that it had inspired him over the years and so sat down and slowly and painstakingly wrote, day after day.

He was cutting and shaping a play out of Franz Kafka's masterpiece *The Trial*. And one day it was finished and all he had to do was find the actors. And lo and behold, one day he did and they were so good, since they were willing to rehearse each night for nothing, and an actor who is willing to work for nothing must be working for love and these are truly the best actors. The actor playing Joseph K., the lead, was perfect for the role even if he had recommended himself for it.

One day after many months of rehearsals, and try-outs and tours they brought their beloved production to the Roundhouse and all was well! He was back in his adored temple and he was, as the expression goes, 'as happy as Larry'.

# 8.

# THE ONE

Dunno how it happened. Grapevine stuff really, since he heard they were casting for a play and checking out actors for a funky one-act curtain-raiser for the main show and the actor they had wanted for it was stuck in Spain filming for the great Orson Welles, who naturally had run over his schedule and so there was a part going that desperately needed to be cast. In fact, there were two roles since the one in the main play had to be performed by the same actor, although it seemed that the curtain-raiser was more important. So he went out and bought the one-act play and thought himself very suited for it and after a few calls to the theatre managed to get himself an audition. Poor Orson Welles. He thought with a certain wryness, "I have always benefited from the mistakes of great men."

So the poor actor who remained in Spain was a reasonably well-known youngish man with a reputation for playing edgy roles, has sadly slipped into the valley of the great unknowns, a predicament feared by all players. Sometimes on sleepless nights one can hear the distinct wailing from that sad pit of iniquity and at such times he'd pull the covers over his head and utter a silent prayer to the great god of actors, Thespis.

He swiftly went out the next morning having secured an audition through much pleading and hustling. Yes, he thought the play *is* quite interesting, dramatic if a tad overwrought, but workable since actors on stage blending and sweating their own lives into a part can seem to cover up a multitude of the writer's quirks and sins. So lo and behold within a couple of days he was called in to 'read' for the part. Oh blessed luck since most time one's pleas are ignored. "Come and read for it," the director said, "tomorrow midday." So he worked on a couple of speeches and worked them pretty hard and felt he might just have some advantage since it was an audition for one of those brutally realistic American plays and as he had a good ear for the American accent and rhythm he believed he had a handle on it. After all, the piece was about a misfit, a loner, a sensitive outsider, looking for, nay begging, for friendship from a world whose values he despises. Neurotic and self-obsessed, oh a bit close, if not more than a bit close; he thought hopefully that this closeness would give him an edge on the others. So the following day he took the tube all the way to this grotty old Victorian theatre deep in London's unfashionable East End.

It was a theatre that was once legendary. Led by a firebrand of a director who seemed to have a rare skill to inspire her actors until they outshone all those stiff West End actors in those awful, horrible plays, where all the sets looked totally alike and the plays were totally obsessed with the same boring and mundane class of people and who played to the audience of the same class.

In this theatre, plays were staged about British working-class life, and full of life as you never before saw on a stage – dynamic, furious, savage and comic and performed by actors who moved like orang-utans, loose, spontaneous and from the hips and he remembered all of them. Remembered the excitement of just going east to see one, since he knew it would be like nothing else he'd ever seen. And the queen, the grand matron, the mother figure, Joan Littlewood was in charge, and she was the guvnor in every sense of the word and she has never been forgotten nor ever will be, while the others will crumble into the dusty filing cabinets of forgetfulness.

He exited from the tube and walked down the narrow street of working-class houses until he arrived at the theatre, which was a magnificent Victorian edifice. He entered the building and before long was talking to the affable director who after the usual polite peregrinations suggested he read from one of the big speeches, which were more like arias. The director led him onto the stage and no matter how many stages you step onto, there is for the actor a strange sense of awe as he stares out into the massive void, where tens of thousands of souls have sat, and laughed or wept as the play's rituals unfold, and he cannot help but experience this feeling since this is an arena where great dramas take place, where reputations are made in a night, or lost. This is a place of life or death.

He began the reading and straightaway knew he had the director's attention, knew it since nobody can read like an actor who slips into a role as easily as into an old suit. He *was* the character since his own tormented life, one might say, overlapped in many areas with the protagonist and there was a strange sense of identification. But the director obviously seeing that here was an actor born to play the role, felt that he didn't wish to show how impressed he really was (the director must never lose power or authority), he asked him to read it once more with a bit more edginess and nervousness.

So of course he did, showing the character as quick to react, cynical, possibly dangerous, and unpredictable. He felt he was 'acting' it out a bit, showing a bit of flashiness, even though he had to do it with the script in his hands, but the director had done what the director does, and that is 'direct', ride the horse, so to speak. The director was pleased and wanted to tell the actor, "Well done, and you've got the job," but not wishing to appear too easy, added that he did quite well and that he would be sure to call him by the next day. Of course he followed through on his promise, and told him the role was his! There was also a smaller role in the second and main play but he felt that he couldn't really do justice to both when the first play had a giant monologue, over five pages long and that was as much as he could reasonably take on in the time. This in no way prejudiced his chances since the director actually thought he was so good in the first one, or at least showed hints of that in the reading, that he would hire another actor for the second and main play.

After he put the phone down he screamed out to no one except the four walls, "I GOT IT!! I GOT IT!!" He was a very happy actor!

Now, as it so happens, he was at the time doing a rather strange job, working as an understudy for two mime artists in a small West End show, and the bizarre thing was that he could not possibly go on for either mime since neither had given him one rehearsal in all the weeks they had been touring. Not one, although he had spent about twenty minutes after much heartfelt requesting, with the more obliging one. So he could never go on, not in a thousand years although he had the skills to do so if he had been taught the routine. They were both very good mimes even if the show was, he thought, a little too commercial and compromised by trying to appeal to too many tastes. It included mime, some singing, and even a bit of dancing. The show was a bit of a pot pourri but he could sit in his dressing room and learn his lines for his next job, and after all it was a peaceful place to work on them and do his fancy 'moves'. He shared his understudy duties with a sweet but rather plain-looking girl who was covering for the women. Before he got his new job he would just sit in the dressing room, feeling quite useless and wait for the second act to start at which time understudies were allowed to go home once it looked like the show was safe.

The theatre was a slightly rundown West End venue that seemed as if any day it might be converted into a cinema or torn down to make room for yet another office block but somehow kept going with plays that couldn't raise the necessary capital for a first-class venue. Sometimes shows that had received great reviews whilst on tour found, as soon as they were thrown into that particular snake pit, that sure enough they slowly suffocated. The actor was only too glad to give in his notice and not to have to turn up any more and sit in the dressing room while the poor cast played to ever diminishing audiences.

Now he was really getting going on that lead role in a one-act play in London that was going to be reviewed by the entire national press! He didn't allow that fact to faze him. He was really just concentrating on the rehearsals which took place in the mornings as the director had to work the main show in the afternoon. Each day he progressed and soon was 'off the book'. Now as fate would have it the stronger he became in the role and the nearer it got to that fateful night the more the vile little worm of angst gnawed into his brain. Doesn't life work in paradoxes since what one wishes for most may suddenly turn up with a vengeance? He had won a role which he had coveted from the bottom of his heart, playing a leading part for the first time in his young life with a first-rate company. Suddenly doubts invaded him from all sides and as one was despatched, another rushed in to take its place, for what one wants and craves so desperately awakens those other areas in the brain. Those are the swamps where the demons lay dormant and are suddenly roused by the fever of your desires and wish to feed on them and to even eventually destroy them. They come in leagues. Fear of losing one's lines, particularly in the middle of that monstrous five-page speech, and with the eyes and ears of the world on you was too horrible even to contemplate; fear that may sap purpose and resolve and even if one was to get through it, one would be uncertain, self-conscious and lose that spirit of abandon which every actor relies on.

How vulnerable is an actor relying purely on memory and willpower and a certain amount of courage to get him through that terrible ordeal, the trial by fire of the first night, the critics out in droves, friends and family out there gritting their teeth, digging their nails into their palms and suddenly, yes suddenly, "Oh God, what comes next!" But strangely some guardian angel nearly always manages to guide actors through, for there seems to be some positive spirit inside them that rarely lets them 'die' on stage. It finds a way to speed through all their neural pathways in a split second to save them. Thank God for that for they must believe in that, but still the fears leak into the fissure and cracks of their poor egos. What a life.

They beg for work and when they actually get it they suffer the angst's of hell!

However, one day he met up with an angelic young actress with whom he had worked a couple of years back in a production of *Hamlet* and in which the lead was played by one of the most brilliant and exciting actors on earth. What an opportunity to study such a marvel of acting technique at such close range! He felt that he had in some way introjected the great actor's style and personality into himself. This often happens with actors who have not yet reached maturity and are still trying to determine what kind of instrument they are and how to hone their instrument to give out the best tones so to speak. The actor's personality is quite often an amalgam of all the parts they have played and so many make the rather strange comment that when they're not 'acting', in other words engaged in a specific personality, they don't really know who they are.

So this great actor's Hamlet, so sleek, so daring, so unpredictable, so brilliant, embedded itself, mind, body and all, and gave him, the young actor, a yet unformed player, a guide, a lesson in how to approach the role … physically, for this great actor was so daringly physical. And when the right role turned up the young actor would simply switch the 'borrowed personality' on. It was on this production when the young lady and he met and occasionally exchanged bodily fluids which gave both of them a kind of intimacy and ease in discussing anything personal.

He confessed to her that though highly excited to be playing this demanding role, and at the same time as suitable for this role as any actor could possibly be, he was still attacked by nerves. In fact a whole effing army of nerves were ambushing him from all directions, and while he rehearsed well, he could put them at bay but it was at night when he lay in bed tossing and turning and sweating that the loathsome acid of fear hacked at his nerve-endings. Yet under all that debris, under all those demons wishing to smother and destroy him was a spirit that he felt was unconquerable, yet the fear still battered at his peace of mind and he wanted release from it. So, confessing his plight to her she said, "I know something that can help you, there's something you can take for that." She spoke of musicians who have to prepare for months for a concert who can be so afflicted with nerves that it paralyses their performance, which under normal circumstances would be brilliant. Actors too with the added stress of a first night often find it impossible to give the true essence of themselves. Now, like a magician, she revealed the secret; a simple pill that one can take to calms the nerves but doesn't affect the performance. "Oh my God. Thank you, thank you my love." He was overjoyed. Perhaps this would spell the end of his torment, and he blessed her and thanked her profusely "Yes, it calms you down," she added, "as long as you don't overdo it." So very grateful for this piece of arcane knowledge, he rushed to his nice, East European doctor who had the habit of calling him "Dollink", and asked him for the magic pill. The good doctor raised a bushy eyebrow but acceded to the request upon hearing of his dire need.

From then on he took one 10mg pill before rehearsal each morning, and yes indeed, it did have the effect of relaxing him beautifully. Oh, that nice soft relaxed feeling, just about fifteen minutes after swallowing. He felt his new 'pal' stomping on all those nerve terrorists but as the days grew closer to that dreaded night the nerves redoubled their efforts to destabilise him and so now he doubled the dose each day and felt the angst once more slip away into the never-never lands. During the last few rehearsals he felt he was getting to grips with a really interesting interpretation, even if it was much coloured by the unique *Hamlet* and maybe the great performer influenced him to make the role just a tad flashier than it really demanded, but it worked and the director seemed impressed and gave very few notes. His fellow actor was calm and perfectly cast in the other role and even so he had a huge lead in the main play. He was an admirable actor who completely submerged himself in the character.

Now the pleasant director had much on his plate and even if the actor thought that the world revolved around him and his great part and in his kind of dreamy pill-induced state it did, however the director explained patiently to him that he still had so much to do with costumes and a complex set and quite a few teething problems. The day of the dress rehearsal came and the nervous actor was desperately keen to play it before the other members of the cast, just to get used to the idea of people watching him. This now was vital to him and even if he feared a professional actor's eye, he knew it was essential to have it. So the day came and he took his two pills and made his way to the beautiful theatre in the sordid and decayed East End.

The nice director reiterated that he would dress rehearse the main play first since it had the complicated set and they needed to see it up and functioning whereas the actor's piece was being played in front of it divided by a backcloth and his bench, which was the only set used, stage-right.

He waited patiently, ran over his big speech a couple more times, had a roll-up, made some tea but after a few hours, an assistant came up to his dressing room and said, "The director is really sorry but he's having such problems that he needs to resolve it and won't get to you today, but promises that he'll run the act, first thing tomorrow." "Tomorrow, on the day we open, the day of the first night!" he thought, "So I won't have the time to adjust to an audience, won't have time to get my nerves steady, as they must be for the first raw exposure to my fellow thespians." His nerves were bound like a spring wound tight and ready to explode and now he had nowhere to discharge them and they seethed, and twisted and ran riot.

Regrettably he was not the kind of person who could take a deep breath and swallow disappointment, and wait for it to settle. It rose in his spleen and his fears rushed across his brain like the darkest furies of hell. He felt betrayed, not just let down but as if some unnameable crime had been committed against him. He didn't know what to do, since he was like a victim of forces way beyond his control. He went downstairs when they were having a small break. He went downstairs with a bellyful of pain, fear, frustration and even madness, and spewed it all out. His mouth and lungs became a vomitorium, he was howling, almost screaming, almost crying. In the beautiful old theatre the agony of a terrified actor was detonated and everybody just stood still and listened. They stood stock still witnessing this bizarre actor few had even chatted to since his period of rehearsal was always at a different time. He howled how he needed this rehearsal just to play it for his colleagues so he might build up his resistance to his nerves that would otherwise crucify him, and when the first salvo of his fury, pain and frustration had been discharged, he flew up to his dressing room and wept like a frightened child.

The director now came up and was sweet and kind and tried to comfort him since he knew some actors are like small minefields and have an explosive power that decent ordinary people rarely express. The director said that "without doubt he would get his 'public' dress rehearsal in the morning" and "not to worry, he was superb in the role, beyond what he had even hoped for." He advised him to try to calm down, that he would be perfect in the role and to go home and relax and have a good night's sleep.

So home he went. He had just one friend in the company, the actor who took over the role he was meant to do in the second play but felt that he could not, and this friend said he'd pop on in later and have a chat and a drink, and that was very comforting. After he left, the actor popped another pill and went to sleep.

# THE ONE

The next day. The day. The vital day. The ultimate day. The day when he would be exposed in London for the first time, to the critics in his best role yet, a tour de force that he was chosen for. So he took the tube to the depths of the East End where the once famous theatre drew the crowds. Now it was run by a couple of keen young men who were trying to keep the lights on. He went down to the theatre having taken two pills … take it easy … don't overdo it. He climbed the stairs and got into his costume, his Yankee khaki pants and black shirt and sure enough within a few minutes a voice on the tannoy asked the actors for the first play to standby for the run-through which the cast were obliged to watch having no doubt been asked by the nice director. He probably said, "look, the poor sod's terribly nervous so let's just be patient and try to help him out."

"Yes," he thought, "that's what he probably said." They watched in silence, with n'ere a sound or a chuckle at the more funny or ironic bits, just sat in silence as if obliged to watch this ego-centric lunatic who shrieked like a virgin before a first night. But he did it and yes, he did feel waves of cynicism flowing over the footlights but it mattered not a jot since he was exposing himself and putting a seal on it so to speak. The rehearsal though felt stiff, self-conscious and even a bit wooden, but he got through it and they clapped politely at the end, and he was very grateful to them. Then he had a few hours until the first performance and so having got through his piece he felt sufficiently purged to be able to watch the other actors run through the main show. He was deeply impressed by the lead actor who was at the same time playing the supporting part in the first play and also impressed that he could do both parts with such apparent ease.

There were still a few hours to go before the 'off' and so he rested in his dressing room, chatted to the actor who shared it with him, a charming comedian with a clown-like face and a tolerant attitude towards his foibles, if not a touch motherly; then he made some tea and worked on his speeches a bit more. His show was the first on. "Take another pill," he thought. That was pill number four but over the whole day and he felt half-relaxed and half-numb. Two hours to go – still feeling edgy and a bit dry – he made some more tea. The actresses in the other show barely even spoke to him but he was used to that and in a way it felt better so he didn't have to deal with them and make polite chat.

An hour to go and suddenly a cold gush of horror went through him as if he was about to face the firing squad. The drug was somehow still holding him in place, floodgates holding the turbulent rivers of his emotion intact. He felt strange, nervous but in control and even dare he think it, a bit sleepy. So maybe just one more, one last pill, and that's enough, more than enough, for what if it had the reverse effect and started nibbling at his memory cells where the precious text is stored? That's a risk but now he felt better, even if he'd taken enough pills to put a horse to sleep. He tried to imagine what it would have been like without them. Impossible. Hysterical, fearful, but now just peaceful. The half-hour was called. He had even nodded off for a few minutes. In the sombre gloom of the dressing room where he sat almost half asleep he heard the 'Five' being called, closed his eyes once more and just let his mind drift; drifting away he actually fell asleep and was only woken by those two terrible words that strike the heart of every actor. "Beginners please." What a call to arms, to face your God, confront the demon, Fear. 'Beginners please' is a command that no actor on earth dares shirk from. No, no, it is a command that you cannot refuse. He just accepted it and rose slowly to his feet and walked steadily down the stairs to the stage, entered it and took his place. He smiled tightly at his fellow actor. They waited for the curtain to rise.

He could hear the banter of the audience who had mainly come for the second play and were mildly curious about the curtain-raiser. He had no friends in – not for a first night – ever. How could he? One cannot make the presumption that one will get through it unscathed. But he did get through it. He started the play. He delivered the first lines and yes the lines came out, blessedly they came and as he saw they were coming, it emboldened him to try and do what he had done in rehearsals – be vigorous, daring and inventive. Now there was laughter, then, there was silence, and then, at the end there was a hearty applause. He had done it. He had more than just got through it. It was all in him ready to be released but it was the magic pills that helped, they gave him ballast, and that steadied him through the storm. God bless his lady friend who revealed the secret of the magic pill.

At the end of the show there was no party and nobody expected it since they just had their friends in, all excited and crowding the dressing rooms of the other actors. He washed his face, and was so, so, so very proud to have got through it. The nice director knocked on his door and said, "Well done, very well done," and then there was another knock and standing there was a beautiful young lady who he saw from time to time: a Swedish girl who he had met at mime class a couple of years ago. He had a friend after all!! And that was quite wonderful since he would have liked nothing better than to have asked her, but asking would have been impossible for him; he had hoped that some friends would just turn up. And she did and nothing could have pleased him more than to see her, beautiful Lisa. He was thrilled that a woman, his woman, had come to see him at his moment of triumph. She confessed that she had been so nervous for him she had to vomit in the ladies room. He found her concern very moving – she was so nervous, so apprehensive for *him*!

Now he could celebrate, he had faced his demons and he had a friend who had been sick with worry over him. Now he could reward himself and that was the best feeling in all the world. He took her to his favourite restaurant in the entire world, a Russian restaurant in Knightsbridge called Luba's Bistro where everything tasted utterly sublime as only food can taste after one is released from the scaffold. After the food and after the wine they walked to his little flat in Pimlico and loved each other and slept in each other's arms.

When he awoke he found that she had already tiptoed out. Shortly after the phone rang. It was she. "The reviews," she said, "were fantastic!!" When he did go out and read them, nearly every one was positive and one or two were even "Fantastic!" He was a very happy actor!

# 9.

# AN UNUSUAL AUDITION

O h yes, yes, yes, he was going to audition for his hero, his idol, the one man he regarded and revered as being above all others, head and shoulders above them all. A man whose work stunned audiences because it went beyond the mere appearance of things and penetrated into the heart, the guts, peeled back the skin to reveal the workings of humanity in all its eloquent profundity and glory.

Audiences went to his productions expecting the unexpected and were never disappointed. He made the art of the actor noble and austere, dignified and respected since he took actors far beyond their usual pale limits. And now this actor had been chosen by the casting agent at the theatre to audition for this giant, since they must have seen something in him, perhaps, detected just that edge of rebelliousness, that glint of the possessed that certain actors have, as if always searching, forever searching for that lodestone that would take them over to the other side. The side where appears the great revelations, the other dimensions. This is the place where few rare actors go – but once they have tapped on those inner doors, tapped on those doors that when opened, reveal such wondrous mysteries that one can never again be the same. How could you be? Only the greats have been there, have made those tremendous inner leaps to where their souls lay waiting to be revealed. They know when they have reached those areas, those magic terrains for then they feel such ecstasy as they have never before felt. All fear, all timidity vanishes for there is something deep within, deep in everyone's core which contains the origins of their being, and how they long to feel it, see it, touch it. Even the great master Olivier one night playing *Othello* dived down deep into those seething depths and once he returned to our world was at a loss as to how he did it.

And the entire cast surrounded him, and praised him and loved him and yet the master was sad and disappointed for he knew not how he had made that incredible journey, knew not the steps he took. The young actor's hero Peter Brook would know, in fact, it was a God-given duty for an actor to take that leap into their own fears, their own doubts, break those limitations and liberate that great bird of one's own imagination.

Now he had been called to the theatre to reveal some of his abilities to the true master of the theatrical universe. And so that morning he spent an hour on his voice, howling, raving, shouting, crying, humming, singing, chanting and then another hour running through all the soliloquies that he knew, that he had performed over and over again for umpteen repertory companies, and he knew so many and so ran through a speech of Hamlet, Henry V, Iago, Oberon, Hotspur, Macbeth, and when he had shot his bolt through all those wonderful characters, he physically warmed up, stretched, did some yoga, which included long stretches of the 'plough' and intense spinal twists, unsupported headstands, handstands, then showered the sweat off, felt quite wonderfully liberated, dressed and then shot off to the great and majestic Old Vic.

He made it to the theatre in good time. He was asked to wait in an adjacent room, which was quite shortly occupied by three other actors, one an attractive girl who he had met at one of those second-rate reps he had worked at in the early days. They all chatted rather excitedly together and of course being Peter Brook and no ordinary director, the group were not going to audition in an ordinary way. They were summoned into a large room.

The master was sitting behind a long bench with about five other members of the staff and the four actors, the happy few, you might say, faced him, feeling both proud to be there and a little like sheep being put through their paces. Peter spoke, as was his way, calmly, to them. He wished to see them work together and set the actors their first task. They were to split into pairs and mime playing tennis together! Oh my gosh, our supplicant thought, this was going to be fun and since he was an adept mime having studied with the mime master Jacques Lecoq, he wouldn't just fall into some sloppy, dopey style of pretending to have a bat in his hand, whilst puffing and panting. The other two were indeed huffing and puffing and panting and when it was the turn of the other pair in which our keen hero was a partner, he whispered to his fellow player, "Go slow … like slow motion" and so they did and he lifted his arm very slowly, threw his imagined ball into the air, watched it sail through space, describe an arc, then descend and now drew back his imaginary racquet and whacked it high in the air following with his eye as it rose, and then returned to his partner's racquet.

His partner hit it dutifully as he was advised

though of course not nearly with as much grace as our trained hero but still good enough for our actor to watch the ball sail through space as if through ether, watched it ever so slowly sink, and even cheekily step back as if to prepare his body, to place his body in the best position to strike the ball again and so he did. And it was very elegant. It was even rather smart, and even one dare say quite beautiful and as he was feeling rather proud of himself the master said, "Thank you" and so they stopped and then heard the next instructions: "Now do it in slow motion!!!" Oh dear, the actor had anticipated the director, was ahead of him, ahead of the game and the director, having seen the actor, wasn't willing to relinquish his thought-out plan, but never mind, why should he, since after all the other two were the puffers and panters and they would have a chance to show *their* dexterity. So they went at it again repeating what they'd already done. "But never mind," he thought, "we'll try and improve on what we did" and so after a few serves the master called for a halt and this time he said, "Now hit the ball only with your voices" Now this was different and so the actors "Poooooooowed" or "Wheeeeeeeeeeed" or "Pop! Po! Pap! Paaaaaaa! Pooooooooo!" And this went on for some little while and our young actor was as reasonably dextrous with his vocal chords as he was with his muscles and sinews. But from the other pair a most bizarre shrieking sound was heard. One of the pair was letting out the kind of piercing sound that martial artists sometimes make just before they strike as if to summon up lightning bolts of courage. This went on for some time and the actor felt, to be perfectly fair, it was an impressive scream although it had little to do with the sound that would suggest symbolically a tennis ball sailing through space. He couldn't even begin to compete with it since it was such a bizarre harrowing sound, which must have been arrived at after many years of fastidious training. Now this seemed to intrigue the master and our intrepid young neophyte who had dared upstage the master was now put in the shade by this weird, blood-curdling shriek.

No, the young actor could not compete with that no matter how valiantly he tried. No matter, he did the very best he could and soon the test was over and all four were exhausted, depleted, and happy to have been put through their paces. They were all asked to wait in the room where they had first met and dutifully, they all marched in and chatted excitedly about what they had been through.

Our young, bold and idealistic actor was proud of what he had achieved and even more satisfied with himself for having spent years working on movement, gesture, mime and felt that he had been fortunate to have learned a language of the theatre and not sozzled himself blotto in pubs which seemed to be the fashion of the young bloods at that time. Even the other actors were suitably impressed and made positive comments on his skill, saying, "it's obvious that he'll want you. It's plain to see that you've had training haven't you Harry". "I wish I had done some more movement after I left drama school ... Where did you go? ... Where did you study?" "Well I ..."

He was just about to modestly answer the question and feel reasonably satisfied with himself when a young lady came into the room. They all stood up. The young lady smiled and said, "Peter wants to thank you so much for coming in and all the effort you put into it. He really appreciated it. And now he'd like you, and you to come back," pointing to the pretty young lady and the man with the blood-curdling shriek, "and the others can go."

He had been dismissed, dismissed by the master. Dismissed. He couldn't get the word out of his head. 'I can go!' He, who was without question the most able of the lot, the most physically skilled was dismissed. He couldn't believe it, could just not effin believe it and even as they were picked out one of them threw him a look as if to say, "Why us and not you?"

He went out into the street, his heart was pounding. Even the other dismissed actor was more concerned about his colleague than himself. "Can't understand that Harry ... but never mind," he thought. "It may be because I was just a tad too cocky, a shade too much ahead of the game, a bit of a know-all. Of course, that was it. He didn't want a cocky smart joker." And no matter how often he tried to understand the great master's rejection of him, it still came back to haunt him. Over and over again he went through his audition like videotape constantly running and rerunning in his head. "Where did I go wrong? Why did he find me so unappealing? And the great director was the master and I would have been such an adoring and willing acolyte. I would have done anything he wished, I would have taken off on the great wings of his imagination, I would have soared, soared high into those rare heights where only the brave and utterly selfless could go since I would be guided by the great master, my hero. My saviour!"

Alas it was not to be and thus, he was cast back onto the dung heap of rejects and returned to feeding on the stale crusts of TV bit parts and the odd stint in some ghastly forsaken rep in some provincial theatre that was sinking into decline and just waiting to be taken over, smashed to the ground so that from the ashes a bright new super-market would rise.

"But does it matter? Think how many auditions you have done," he thought, "and how many times were you not quite right, since you cannot begin to know or to understand what goes on in the director's head. For directors, like actors are also vulnerable even though they may have to act like generals in charge of their troops, taking them into battle, guiding, training, inspiring, teaching even. But they still must feel totally secure and unafraid of what comes before them. Be secure in their choice of human cargo so that they may mould and shape, inspire them to great heights and at the end of the day to be admired, yes, just a little admired and respected, and even to be loved. To be loved and not have to face down a snotty-nosed know-all who thinks he's oh so smart, so savvy and may, yes may know a little too much for his own good."

All these thoughts went on a rampage through his brain, twisting and turning themselves inside out trying to solve what was becoming a riddle in the poor actor's mind. He had to stop these ruminations, stop these errant thoughts that bombarded him like the shattered fragments of a meteorite. He still admired his master, his beloved master who had spurned him, who had turned away the one person who would have so faithfully not only served but also carried out his will with the dedication of a Samurai who would not hesitate to commit hara-kiri when his Lord passed away. Of course, he would still love and respect his master and faithfully attend his shows, never ever missing one. And in the meantime the cast, without the loyal actor who had auditioned with such zeal, went to work. Rumours flew out from the rehearsal studios since actors carry gossip and spread it faster than plague victims. The strange exercises the cast were induced or even obliged to do, the lengthy rehearsal time, which of course also suggests the profundity of the piece, its great ambition and scale.

While the young actor had now put his pain, his hurt and frustration that he was not there with them to the back of his mind, he still envied those who had the opportunity to be working, nay creating in that temple of light. All those actors breathing in the atmosphere of great art and all of them, each of them better than he. But never mind, he thought, there may be another time in the future. Another moment to approach the master and beg to be a disciple.

Meanwhile the months passed and he continued to do a part-time job of teaching earnest students in a backwater drama school, which at least paid his wages and even allowed him to do some experiments of his own.

One day in the press, he saw a notice that the production, the master's great new work was about to be exposed at the grand old theatre and since tickets were reduced for the previews he rushed to the box office and bought himself a precious ticket, an expensive one even for a preview, but he was glad, so very glad since he so adored those rare events when the master revealed a new work.

Of course it would be disingenuous to believe that the young man's interest was purely to satisfy his aesthetic taste buds. No, it would be fair to admit that he wished to see the calibre of the cast the master had carefully chosen and for whom he had been so cruelly cast aside – just to satisfy that still nagging pain in his ego. Then he would feel vindicated in his belief that some sort of agenda was at work and would question no further. And if they were superb and stood out obviously as theatrical athletes he would not only be happy but would use the opportunity to drive himself harder and further and curse himself for not having done so in the past with the zeal necessary to capture the attention of those whose standards are not those of ordinary men.

He waited as expectant as he always was when

facing the master's work. The staging was mini-malistic. The actors sat on small cubes in a semicir-cle and delivered their well-written speeches with vigour and expressiveness. They passed sounds to each other with expert and precise timing and he followed the play extremely well since it was writ-ten by a dazzling writer who was also a poet as well as a playwright. He, of course, could not help noticing that a few of the players were chained to pillars in the auditorium and even gave a sigh of relief since he might not have wished to stand half-naked tied to a pillar and being part of a human orchestra. "Ah," he thought, "perhaps the master was trying to save me since having observed me as one who could acquit himself well was reluctant to have me tied to a pillar." The poor leading man seemed most unsuited to the role even if he was one of England's great knights. It looked like he had come out of the wrong play and wandered into this one by mistake. Still the production had some sweep and verve but dare he admit it, even to himself, that it wasn't quite on the level of his last masterworks. Perhaps the young actor was deter-mined not to be too impressed, not to be amazed, lest his anguish at being left out was too much to take. But no. He sat calmly watching and admiring even if his admiration was beginning to cool just a bit. Those exercises were just too familiar that the master was using so expertly, and now he was waiting patiently for the end. But then! Oh yes, but then... Taking his place on one of the cubes was the actor with the splendid scream, that howl that seemed to come up from nowhere and apropos of nothing very much, he once again let out that same blood-curdling screech. That's all he seemed to do all evening, apart from sometime joining in the vocal orchestra.

Now, had the scream meant anything, or was it a reaction to some horrendous piece of news then it might have been justified, but no, it just hung there like a piece of 'biz', some 'shtick'. And now the young rejected actor was almost glad that he was rejected. The master was actually trying to spare him the anguish. Or was the young fellow just stretching his negative interpretation of the event so far that it covered his pathetic underused being. However what followed next was indeed so bizarre that he could scarcely believe his own eyes. What followed was so strange, so out of joint that one might be forgiven for thinking that the master had lost those beautiful marbles that jangled around his inventive brain and replaced them with dog turds.

No, that was too severe an interpretation. The young actor was just rudely seizing on anything that was just too eccentric and clinging to those 'flaws' as his ultimate justification; his belief that he was better off not being cast, and was spared. Phew! And thank God! But at the play's end was wheeled on stage a huge object covered with a cloth of some kind. The audience waited in anticipation for some further revelation from the talented master and they did not have to wait long. The cloth was suddenly pulled swiftly off and there, centre stage was a massive golden cock! A shiny great golden cock and if this was not quite enough, music was struck up in a kind of Dixieland style so favoured by those middle-class students in roll-neck sweaters whose taste was anathema to lovers of modern cool jazz sounds.

Frankly, not only could our young actor not believe what he was seeing, but was struck so deeply by a wave of revulsion that it seemed to saturate his whole being. It was horrific. Not obscene, not just vulgar, which could have valid aesthetic points, but what was revealed by this act was some deep-seated insecurity in his revered master. An insecurity so deep and so vast, as if he wished, so desperately wished, to be 'bold', 'daring', 'outrageous' like those dazzling crazy lunatics in New York, 'the Living Theatre' to whom he had snuggled up to so eagerly.

"And for this, for this I was rejected!" Suddenly something stirred inside his being as if a monster had just incubated within him. He felt this thing, this incubus within him and then, in the middle of the theatre the air inside his lungs burst out and his vocal chords let out a howl that reverberated round the entire auditorium: "RUUUUUUUUUUUBBBBBBBBBBBISHHH!!!"

He swiftly exited. On the tube home he did feel a little pleased with himself but also realised that the opportunity to work for his most admired master was probably now shot down in flames. A shame really.

# 10.

# THE ARTS LAB, DRURY LANE

Years ago, in fact in the Sixties in London, there was such an inordinate desire to express oneself that this desire translated itself into a phenomenal growth of theatres. They sprouted up in every nook and cranny, attic, crevice, basement, warehouse; and therefore every actor, writer, director, who felt that they did nor fit into the conventional, hidebound, self-regarding ho-hum establishment could find some small sanctuary to blow hard and practice their art, no matter how strange, weird, bizarre, non-conformist, sexy, violent, or simply crazy. This place, this sanctuary, this home, even, was like a temple where, no one within reason was refused a place to rest their head, or rather stand centre stage and express their spirit and the sighings of their soul. Here the growing guilt of unemployment would not eat away at the performer's marrow and ego until it became nigh on impossible to believe in himself.

Of course an actor desperately needs to perform in order to practice that most elusive of art, and that mysterious genie of inspiration is not likely to appear unless one is, you might say, 'cooking' in front of an audience. One needs to toughen those psychic muscles and nerves by frequent exposure before one's peers, since without that, the flesh may become too soft and too easily penetrable by the nasty barbs of doubt. And yet how wearying is all this constant begging and cajoling, hoping for an audition to come up to be performed in front of some moon-faced loon who is standing in for his lazy and indifferent master. So after practicing your pathetic audition pieces you might have to expose yourself to some dullard assistant, some underling whose duty it was to fulfill the quota of auditions required by the actors' union, Equity.

The young actor's routine was, more or less, to write daily to nearly every repertory company in Great Britain, to frequent the gym, the old and comforting YMCA on Tottenham Court Road; where many fellow actors also did their physical duties so that they might be ready and in good condition when informed that they would be seen for a job. And when he had performed his much-practised party pieces and the director actually says yes!! Hallelujah! The actor, on one occasion having heard from his agent that he'd been accepted, was unable to contain himself, he could not stand up but had to roll on the floor and howl out his delight. Oh heaven, oh joy, oh bliss. He was in nirvana.

But then the season comes to an end but you know that the memory of that time will be emblazoned in your mind forever, until the day you die, for that will have been a special time in your life; and of course, you will remember the romances, the charming little digs that you stayed in, the local Chinese restaurant you always ate in, and the director who is no longer here but whom you once loved, for a benevolent director can so easily become a father figure, since you wish always to please them.

So when the season comes to an end and even if there is no work immediately to follow you are still able to nourish yourself for several weeks or even months on the memory of those times, like a hedgehog feeding on its stored layers of fat during the bleak winter times. There were so many nights, some thrilling, some less so, and those nervous first nights when still vulnerable to those irrational fears that always seem to find a way of slipping through your defences. But hey! You did it, and you had a couple of precious months, that during the following barren times would manage to keep you fed. Keep you nourished while you hibernated, only you didn't hibernate, you went back on the treadmill and hustled and bustled and kept your ear on the grapevine, that extraordinary actor's telepathic service where news travels fast, very fast.

However, something was happening, something was moving in the city, small shoots were breaking through the cracks in the city's façade, and exotic and unknown fruits were emerging, no doubt spawned by the recent outbreak of a completely new and unknown form of bacteria; the flood of radical American drama. Intrepid adventurers saw that what could be expressed on stage was just about fifty times stronger than had been exhibited limply on the English stage for the past fifty years. Works that were shocking, moving, dynamic, personal, intimate were let loose and the wide eyes looked on in awe and amazement as if witnessing monstrously exotic creatures that had hitherto been thought of as extinct.

These works galvanised the audiences as if a bolt of electricity had been fired from the stage and at the end of the evening they staggered out onto the street, never to forget what they had seen. Now, dotted round the city were these nests, theatrical nests, small, sometime grimy venues that were incubating the bastard offspring of their American seducers. Sometimes the plays were spat out if not shat out! One day the young actor wandered into one of them, an avant-garde arts lab in Drury Lane. A lab in which to experiment, a place to reveal the soul of mankind, to try the kind of things that would never see the light of day or the stars at night for that matter in other ghastly theatres that were really mausoleums.

One day, when the pain, the angst, the sourness, that comes when unemployment curdles one's precious life, when each day was less a gift from God than a sentence, he decided to create his own play. Then, having completed this work he took his slim one-act play in his hands and walked into this strange building, called 'The Arts Laboratory'. There was a large long room which seemed to be a general reception area for milling around or drinking coffee in and there always seemed to be people doing this, quite guiltlessly and happy to be skiving around with no particular purpose in life, their brains no more than squatting inside their skulls. There was a large room to the left, which was the performance space which could seat about sixty spectators on one side which gave the room a long rectangular feel. It was a good space and certainly had atmosphere. So he went in and met the young and rather cool creator of the Lab, an American,

Jim Haynes, who had virtually kick-started the first fringe theatre in Scotland called The Traverse. To get to it you had to traverse several flights of rickety stone steps to its premises on the Royal Mile. It was worth it, however, one made the journey, since it housed some of the best drama to be seen in Edinburgh. But Jim Haynes had upped sticks and opened this formidable hothouse in Drury Lane.

So he went in and Jim, remembering how enthusiastic the actor was from his last visits to Edinburgh, was cordial and when he heard about the play he said he wished to stage it, which was most encouraging. The young actor explained the nature of the play which was harrowing in more ways than one. Basically it was a straightforward adaptation of a Kafka short story and this appealed to Jim who was as far away from what currently excited the shrivelled loins of British drama as the actor was. So he suggested that Kafka's brilliant, nightmarish and satanic horror story, *The Penal Colony* would be most appropriate for the Art Lab, to which Jim readily agreed. The story was about a machine of execution that performed its honourable task of killing the condemned man by writing his 'sentence' on his back, effectively tattooing him to death. The climax of the story is when the condemned man suddenly realises that the sentence is written on his back and struggles to read it despite the pain. Eventually he understands it, and that is the climax for which the audience has gathered.

Jim liked the story so much that he suggested there and then a performance date, which was just a couple of months ahead in May, and it was left like that. Now it was up to him, the actor, to recruit some good dependable actors and after making some soundings here and there made his decision. Alas, his unfortunate natural shyness caused him some difficulty in confessing to his future employees that *he* would be playing the lead role of the commanding officer as well as directing it and being responsible for the adaptation. So he began rehearsals and though awkward at first, he readily understood that what propels one to achieve anything is the need to conquer those nasty doubts and fears. The actual act of doing propels one forward, as if some kind of propane gas was produced as a by-product, and thank God for that.

Nevertheless, as fate would have it, one actor left and then another and he was on the point of thinking about cancelling his cherished project when he received some ghastly news. His beloved lady was diagnosed with some dreadful malaise and was due for extensive tests, and suddenly nothing seemed to matter or have such importance as this and all his woes shrunk into petty nothingness. The actor swore to God that if she recovered, he would never again hesitate or prevaricate, or give in at the first doubts but go straightforward and achieve what he had set his heart on. Her recovery was even swifter than the doctors had imagined and soon she was declared totally fit. His relief was so great that he decided to overcome all problems, vanquish all fear and get on with it at all speed.

But now, as director, he needed what was to be the centre image of the story and that was an execution machine of diabolical design if it was to in any way approximate Kafka's uncannily detailed description. By the blessings of his good lady he had acquired friends of a higher calibre than hitherto he had felt himself to be worthy of, and one of these was an architect by the name of Alistair, who was not only skilled as a draughtsman but was a carpenter of astonishing virtuosity. Alistair read the short story and agreed to make the execution bed according to the infinitely detailed description by Franz Kafka.

To take on such a work would be nigh on impossible and horribly expensive but our young, brilliant, and daring architect-carpenter went to work and in a few weeks he called the actor to say that the first stages of the machine had been made and would he like to come down and examine the bare bones, which he did with great anticipation. It was incredible, to say the least, and beyond anything that he could have possibly imagined. It was gigantic and made out of the finest pine, sanded, chamfered and beautifully finished. The huge lid that was closed onto the back of the poor victim was pierced with a bed of fine nails to represent the needles and all that was missing was the transparent tubing to transport the blood from the victim and another tube to transport the water, to wash the wound. This would keep the image clear. Oh! The actor was immensely proud. The day came to have the machine transported to the Arts Lab on Drury Lane and a van was hired with some removers to carry it. Jim Haynes was waiting with some curiosity since they'd told him when it was due to arrive.

The cool demeanour that Jim Haynes always seemed to adopt, dropped away, replaced by utter astonishment at this rather tentative actor, since that is how he saw him, who had even blanched when he saw on the Arts Lab wall a poster advertising *his* play confirming that it was really happening on such and such a date, and there was no way out. In his mind, the poster made any postponement impossible as if it was written in blood. Now, proudly, the actor and the architect came into Jim's fringe theatre with a piece of work that could grace any stage in the land.

Once inside the building, Alistair carefully added the theatrical bits and pieces like the tubes for carrying the blood, pipes and electrics for the pulsing lights, the fixed gag for the prisoner's mouth and lo and behold, the play aided by his splendid group of actors began to live. On the night that was determined by the poster, the play came to life for so it does when the first audience comes in. In a way the first audience seals and blesses the play. This was the actor's very first production and no one could have been more proud for this was the beginning.

# 11.

# INSTINCT

In the theatre you might just find that the director has formed an image in his head of how the
role must be interpreted before the actor has
had a chance to rehearse, and rehearsals are the
methods which the actor uses to get the appropriate bells ringing. This is the neophyte director's
trusted way of working, of reading the script and
coming to a conclusion so that he or she can come
to rehearsal and at least appear to be ahead of the
game. The director is not trusting instinct, that
wonderful powerful mechanism, that biological
radar that actors can draw on effortlessly. Instinct
is the ability to draw on the infinite number of
memories stored in the psyche that somehow are
released in times of danger or stress and therefore
are a kind of survival mechanism. An actor must
be able to call upon instinct at lightning speed

since the danger that exists to the ego is quite formidable. The naked actor is thrust into a spotlight in front of what must be millions of faces over a lifetime, and instinct protects the actor from destruction by guiding him and by summoning up a limitless bank of impressions. These instincts, carefully selected and then discarding at the speed of light also allow the actor to have insights. The vulnerable rely on instincts to a remarkable degree. But while the director no doubt has talents, they will never be tested in quite the same way as those of an actor. Since they are not, nor ever will be in the firing line of the audience where the instincts are then more than likely to come into play. Unfortunately many of our leading directors, not having put themselves into the spotlight that is the nightly ritual of actors, have not had a chance to develop those instincts which are a part and parcel of the actor's reflex actions, also defence mechanisms.

But it is true to say that they do have an instinct for self-preservation since they are responsible for the outcome like a captain leading his troops into battle and have to face the consequences if their campaign fails, but it is doubtful that this could be called instinct at all. Theatre is unique in this since among all the arts except film, it is the only one where a non-trained person will seek to guide a trained artist. This would not be acceptable if for example a boxer allowed himself to be guided by a non-boxer, or a dancer be choreographed by a non-dancer, or a singer be trained by a non-singer and these examples could go on and on. But in the theatre, it is considered quite normal for a director who has never acted in his life to be given the responsibility of directing a group of actors who will listen obediently and do what he or she asks of them.

There are a rare few directors who have studied their craft so consummately that they are able to shape the play and often with exceptional results. But in the large majority of cases, no instinct can be seen at work, instead, one sees the results of many hours and weeks of plodding research which is a substitute for the instinct that they so sorely lack. They research omnivorously since this at least throws some quite fascinating if useless light on the play, since the author has already drawn on the mass of material he or she has discovered and since the play is the fruit of all of this why is it then so necessary to dig up the research all over again. The answer is in the play itself. When you eat a fruit do you laboriously attempt to discover which plot of land the seed of the fruit was sown? I think not, but the director feels that by attempting to research all the sources of the play he is uncovering valuable information which will magically shed light on the work itself. Rather than shedding light, it more often weighs the actor down with masses of useless information which he is forced to digest but it does not give the actor playing Hamlet one single insight of how to use his voice or body, let alone his mental faculty. The information he needs is all in the work. For a student of literature this mass of research might be of great value in writing up his thesis for a doctorate but he is not having to act it out. Few if any opera singers do this. They merely study the score and understand the character from the emotion in the music and the text. That's all they need. They really don't need to know the life history of Wagner to perform the role of Brunhilde.

The director believes he is giving a service as he sits there bloated with information on the laws of usury in Venice in the sixteenth century. The origins of the word 'ghetto' may be of passing interest but only if it helps the actor into his role. What it does do is put the director in the central spot where he has the attention of the actors. Meanwhile he waits for instinct to surface but it seldom does because instinct has not been called upon and it will not suddenly float above the director's head like an exotic butterfly. The director wishes quite naturally to show why he has been chosen to direct the play and the more he spurts his 'knowledge' which he has spent many weeks laboriously hoovering up, the more he feels the cast will respect him. But the reverse is most often true. The cast begin to tire of him since actors have a burning need to get on their feet and 'move' the play. They want to seize the initiative and move into the battle lines so that they may get in touch with their nerves, with their reflexes, with their skills and most of all with their instinct. This, the director gradually crushes as the actor is forced to sit, to listen, to pay attention, to absorb, to become more anxious, to squirm in his seat while the director raves on and on and on.

Eventually, after a day or two, or more, or even weeks spent doing idle exercises, playing 'games', performing some childish improvisation they may start to slowly plot the play but the joy of doing so has already been sucked out of it and the going will be tough, but with a skilled assistant, choreographer, dance or fight arranger, some semblance of a production may emerge. This has been a hallmark of British theatre for many years and being so, the critics will give it a four-star review since it fulfils the main requirement of Brit theatre and that is that you can at least hear the actor.

There was an actor highly respected for his unusual skills and dynamic approach who was obliged to sit for a month while the director pissed about with his theories. Since they were doing the 'Scottish' play he brought in other experts on witchcraft. For four weeks this director, working for a major company, buggered about while the actors became more and more impotent and frustrated. Eventually he did get around to plotting it and the actor who was one of the country's best, gave the worst performance of his life! Why do they do this? One suspects they mean well but it is a kind of fear, an evasion, a reluctance to face the task of putting actors on stage and experimenting, trying things out, making a decision and then seeing what may strike sparks. They are so afraid of failing that they avoid that decision for as long as possible since what they know and trust are the notes that they have copied down.

To put actors on stage right from the beginning would be more than they could dare and yet this would be the very thing that would force the instinct into play. To be daring. To risk. Actors come to life once they are put on a stage. Once they are standing on a stage an almost alchemical process takes place. In fact, the actors will take command guided by their instincts and the director should heed this for the actor will guide him into the play's labyrinths and enable him to stage it. They're the canaries in the mine that will sniff out the key elements and know or sense what is right for them and what is deeply wrong, but sitting on a chair is wasting their energy and their vital uses.

When a director with strong, inventive and innovative instincts appears on the scene they will certainly delight for a while by demonstrating how fascinating theatre can be but soon they will be summarily dismissed and rarely be seen of or heard of again. Those who rock the boat are never too popular with those who prefer a smooth uneventful crossing. Now this instinct or gift, or special ability, let us say, for summoning up unique and dynamic forms of theatre is not the province of an elite group of genius directors, it is more the province of quite simple and normal people who have studied the art of performance mostly by being a performer. Performers are curious about other art forms like dance, movement, acrobatics etc. and the benefit for the actor of learning these skills is that these techniques will act as support systems whenever a solution is needed or an exceptional idea wanted. The techniques filter themselves into whatever they are doing. Sometimes they are just summoned unconsciously to see if they will enhance the material. Also the actor will be obliged when confronting the audience to put himself into a life or death situation and his instinct is put on high alert in such situations. It's life or death for the ego and that is a perilous time but instinct will nearly always see you through.

However the person for whom the instinct of genius has seldom knocked, or has even needed to knock is nevertheless incredibly protective of their territory, which is to say their status in the world. They will seldom allow a person of instinct a chance to work in their hallowed institutions since such dangerous gifts as instinct are regarded as life threatening or unreliable and must be kept far away. Just to demonstrate a sense of fairness they might allow such a person a crack at the whip every ten years or so. However, their dull coevals who share the same value system will be seen directing quite regularly; even if they rarely set the house alight they are regarded as fairly reliable.

Since the instinctive director still has to work, he foolishly will continue to write polite letters to artistic directors offering exciting ideas and plays but these will be dismissed with a polite answer that the theatre is fully booked for the next year or two and they certainly can't meet since they are always in rehearsal but always politely add that they wish your project well. This may go on for year after year after year and yet the person of instinct has not heard the penny drop and does not know that the kind of instinct that produces inspiring, irrational and non-conformist ideas is anathema to those who have none. The penny has not dropped and he will go on, sometimes even begging for a chance to show his or her work in the hope that the administrator might relent, since the person of instinct is unable to believe in the malice, jealousy and vindictiveness of those who are bereft of it.

There may be an occasion when a rather more flexible artistic director will allow the outsider a brief exposure but then he is sent on his way to struggle in the wilderness and rely on the generosity of foreign arts festivals whose organisations are usually run by administrators who search out imaginative works, since not being practitioners themselves they have nothing to fear from them. So the world is largely divided along those lines.

Now it is curious that the state-subsidised theatre might be the only institutions on earth that actively shuns such people and not only shuns but even discourages, blocks, prevents as far as possible their work from being seen by an audience that may actually crave it and demand it. Therefore you could say that their tax pounds, for which they subsidise the large theatres, are being siphoned off by the establishment for their own purposes and are therefore being defrauded.

As a result one has to, paradoxically, search out the 'commercial' sector, who just like people in industry are always looking for innovators but the fly in the ointment is that they cater to a mass audience that love to stare at stars in the flesh, but if one can negotiate past that one finds that the commercial producer is at least reasonably honest and truthful and their only criterion is the box office, if you can put bums on seats and thank god for that.

One might find strange unedifying echoes of this in countries ruled by dictators. No one is more fearful of change, free speech, spontaneity and individualism than a dictator. They will not tolerate free thinkers or innovative radical theatre directors. They rule with the iron fists of fear and intimidation and people with imagination and instinct fill them with horror and they can go as far as to exile troublesome artists, and in the case of the USSR actually murder them as they did to the great expressionist director Mayakovsky and the master writer Gogol.

But the principal is not so very different here in the West. It too crushes out any man or woman whose instincts do not conform to the procrustean bed of his wretched pedestrian master.

# 12.

# YOU'RE A FILM ACTOR!

**P**oor film actors! It's astonishing what you have to put up with on film to fit your small bits of creation into the whole when the camera and lights are on you, and the director is ready for a take, but until that time happens you sit in a trailer and wait. How long you wait may depend on the previous shots and actors working smoothly and your call for work is based just upon that. But it rarely does go smoothly since the director can never anticipate what chance demons and gremlins will somehow infiltrate themselves in the works. However, you can't be called until they have finished the shot, when you must be made up, costumed and ready to go.

So you sit in your room or trailer or even in your honey wagon, so called since it is a long trailer with several small rooms like a honeycomb and these honey wagons are for the smaller-part actors whereas the more mature or well-known actors will be given a pleasant trailer, which has a bed, a sink, a TV (rarely works) and your own private toilet. Only honey is not what you make in your honey wagon.

Now as we all well know the wages you get on film are not for working but for the endless waiting. You do the work for free, according to Sir Michael Caine and he's not far off the truth. Actors of course have become very resourceful in using the time that they may have to wait. They somehow expect it and it is doubtful if there is any other profession on earth whereby the actual workers have to wait so long merely to do their job, and work. One can't imagine a bricklayer turning up and being asked to wait until the plumber has finished before he can lay a brick. They somehow coordinate. It's a pity that film companies can't do something similar. Some do by having a second unit so the actor can at least be active while the stars are working but that is quite rare. In response, film actors are very resourceful and bring into their trailer all sorts of things to usefully pass the time.

BlackBerrys, iPods, laptops, this techno para-phernalia takes some organising and getting used to. Many debates are held between trailers on how *this* modem works against *this* one and how many thousand songs, tunes, albums you can store on *this* disk and so it goes on everlasting, and oh what fun. How satisfied are the actors as they open the wondrous lid on their silver laptops and joyfully receive all the squiggles and colours and graphics and messages that this miracle of technology has been engineered to send, like 'Have a great day love' from some far-off partner. This is better than a simple phone call since you can stare at the message and reply somewhat pithily rather than be subjected to the exhausting ordeal of actually speaking spontaneously. Then there is the extreme joy of linking all your various toys together into one cosmological nightmare of a machine and with your digital camera taking snaps that can be downloaded onto your laptop and then sent home, which of course necessitates the need of having at least two laptops if not more, for when your kids grow up they will greedily demand every possible gizmo on the market to be like mum and dad.

And so, after all the juggling with buttons, switches, plugs, batteries, hard and soft drives, iPods, emails on the laptops the actor could only wonder at the genius of modern man. He sometimes saw them sitting, even on the set with a laptop poised on their laps, their testicles slowly being irradiated and their sperm sterilised by the toxic beam being discharged. No matter. This actor had just a notebook and a beautiful old fashioned film camera that he liked and could patiently wait to get to London and take them into Quick Print Services which always did an excellent job and then he would show them to his missus which was so much more of a surprise and joy to both of them since neither had seen them before. He had never used a laptop in his life and even confessed to a little pride at airports, when asked if he was carrying a laptop could swiftly respond with an emphatic "No!" He was even proud that he was not cast as one of those loonies who are forever staring into that screen. No!

No, he doesn't carry everywhere one of those intrusive monsters that the entire world seems to take into lovely coffee shops, where once customers read the daily paper or a book, or even occasionally jotted down a few pithy words into a notebook, and how nice is that, to be with your friendly note-pad recording your observations of the day. But today, actors make sure that they are able to fill in the time with lots of playthings and with all these instruments that they can manipulate, they feel to a certain extent, fulfilled and active.

Eventually they will be hauled onto the set to do some execrable dialogue. Sometimes the stuntman, employed if there's the slightest need for the actor to do anything beyond getting up or sitting down, might ask an actor with whom he is not yet acquainted if they do 'dialogue' as if they are reluctant to call what the poor players do as 'acting'. No, it is merely 'dialogue', as if that's all acting is, – just remembering 'dialogue'. There is so much time between takes while the photographer 'checks the gate', lest there's a 'hair in the gate' or the soundman complains of an intrusive noise coming through from a distant plane or a multitude of other things. So actors rabbit, they chatter like no other breed on earth, they chatter like their lives depend on it. They simply have to define who they are! So they go at it with a will and it is as natural as breathing since when you are not acting, where are you and who are you? You cease to exist. You are in limbo land. You're not laying a brick, or cutting a piece of cloth, or teaching a child, or sweeping the street, you are virtually doing nothing so you must chatter and a kind of competition goes on as to who is the most informed, the loudest, the cleverest, the wittiest, the most bombastic, opinionated, smug, rebellious, cynical. You must define yourself!

The actor once worked with an American of the old film school who had established a poker game whenever they were off stage so to speak. The poker became so exciting that they could all barely get back to work when they were called and sometimes the pot became so big that if it hadn't been won before being called to on set, the second assistant would have to wait a few minutes for the hand to be completed.

Alas that wonderful comic, crazy wonderful man is no longer with us. He was on a film where a once mighty English star was declining into a soporific nuttiness, but wished to hold onto his aura and his sense of self-belief. To do this, he 'acted' out his stardom at every possible moment, behaving as starrily demanding as possible. He noisily drew attention to himself at all times and for all things and 'chatted' louder than anyone and made comments to his neighbour who would be obliged to listen with an agreeable grin on his supplicating face as if, oh my dear, how outrageous you are! And so still spreading the wings of his old and battered reputation like some scruffy old peacock he reminded everyone of it even if he was chiefly remembered for one great role in a classic film which is shown on late-night TV more times than can be reasonably tolerated. The old star did make some other films and while some were indeed charming they seemed no more than an extension of his life as a public piss-artist.

The few times the star did appear on stage he achieved a great deal of success, especially in the role of a very public boozer and then he kind of petered out, so to speak. But what he was chiefly known for was his magnificently eloquent voice and from time to time he summoned up that trumpet to convince all around that he was still the king of some remote distant kingdom. On set he would unspool himself running through his life, playing little incidents, despatching old enemies, slaying dull adversaries or singing the praises of colleagues who had long turned into a sour fertiliser for the earth and ruthlessly piercing those old and still living enemies who had crossed him with a long acidic stream of invective. Sometimes the tape got twisted on its spool and he retold stories he had vented only two days before but he told them with such a passion as if relayed for the first time.

He would enter the set, aided by a companion since he was suffering the effects of old age compounded by a life of splendid alcoholic indulgence on a scale that would have killed several oxen. But once ensconced in his comfortable chair felt it mandatory to comment on everyone and everything that was going on in front of him with a kind of playful sarcasm. So this was how the day kicked off for him. This was no longer the set, this was his private club where he sounded off in the way the master in his country house berates the staff (affectionately of course).

"Oh who's wearing a rather spiffy leather

jacket this morning?" and the recipient of his comments would blush and giggle and grin but in a way to show such gratitude that 'Sir' had made him the subject of his withering sarcasm. And to first assistant, "That's a funny haircut, did your wife do it?" The assistant would collapse in a heap of snorts and vainly tried to defend himself but against that great stentorian voice your own sounds feeble and impotent. To a passing young woman doing the props, "Oh you're a very pretty girl, darling, I might have to carry you orf," elicits more giggles, squeaks and blushes and of course, benign smiles from everyone who have involuntarily become the master's audience. Perhaps after his first great role and his instant acceleration into the fiery heights he was burnt up just a little too soon.

Sometimes just going on to the set before you actually start work can be exhausting. You can so easily fall into the habit that non-workers do or shall we say actors, of meeting and greeting and before you are aware of it you are chatting like a monkey on speed, fooling around, telling stories of previous encounters. In fact, you are merely filling in the details of your life as if you were a children's colouring book that shows images in just their outlines and the child is expected to colour it in to breathe life into it. Meanwhile, the real workers have arrived and the director, the photographer, focus puller, soundman, are working non-stop. The film's star has now arrived and takes over with tales of when so and so got pissed, etc., etc. but at least we can rehearse for the camera. The star, just to show that he is on the ball and not just a legendary rip-roarer, questions the cameraman about the size of the lens as if that knowledge will be immediately acted upon and is vital to the construction of his character of which he can scarcely remember the lines. But perhaps it's useful if you're told it's a huge close up and then you will be very still and concentrated – supposedly.

Then once again you're released to your cell where you can catch up on some reading, play on your BlackBerry in which case you never write letters any more. That's a past life. Belonging to another era.

But this is a shorter break and you are called onto the set and brace yourself for the camera. You rehearse and wait for that word 'action'. For some reason, and many leading actors do this, the star lets out a huge barking fit, clearing his throat and it sounds like the Hound of the Baskervilles but this is meant to shake him up and put him into the mood. The actor tries to imagine what would happen if all the cast did that. It would sound like an insane asylum or the zoo but somehow it's expected of the star. Naturally, none of the other actors would dare do this.

Shooting begins: "Sound rolling, speed," says the soundman, "Action," shouts the director. The most magical word in the world. And the simplest. The electronic clapper moves in and now what you have been waiting for, what you have trained for, what you have lived for has now come to pass. The director shoots the scene three or four times unless he's a lunatic or a genius and then it's over and you're relieved, tear off your costumes, wash off your make-up and if on location, hope it's not too late for a pleasant unrushed dinner at the hotel … but who with … who will accompany you? The other actors are still working on the scene that you have exited, so you go back alone to your hotel room and pour a stiff drink … you go down to the dining room for supper and sit alone with a book which is at least peaceful and suddenly you wish it were all over, but this is what you're being paid for, so swallow it and belt up … you're a film actor!

# 13.

# ON THE SET

It was a night shoot. This always made him feel exhausted, particularly about 2 a.m. if he was on standby in his dressing room and knowing he had at least four hours to go. But hell, he was working and earning and having to hang around hour after hour is what he got paid for ... for walking through a sea of turds. He reminded himself to keep that in mind.

You may have to hang around for hours, sometimes days in the worst-case scenario, or be called on the set before you're needed, so try to avoid the endless, mindless yakking that film actors indulge in, try to avoid the temptation of the snack trolley, and hide away in your room and attempt to make use of all the time that is suddenly in your hands.

Eventually you will be called onto the set, desperately trying to shake the sand out of your eyes and do a line-up which is a loose rehearsal for the cameraman to block out his moves and plot the lights to cast his spell on the performance area. If it's your first day or night you will be eyed up suspiciously by the rest of the crew who have an innate distrust of all actors, except of course the stars who they seem to fawn on, since they measure their status against them. Then the star enters and for a few moments he or she is quite charming but after a few takes, if female, will barely talk to you, and even if you share a scene either of some intimacy or violence she may treat you as being more worthless than a cockroach that she would be happy to step on. Perhaps because the film set is so dominantly male she protects herself by withdrawing into her own world. Let me tell you that being shunned hour after hour is not a pleasant feeling … but hey, that's showbiz. After every shot the small supporting staff, the dressers, make-up, stunt organisers, third assistants will all gather round her smiling, waving, patting, smoothing, smooching, powdering and the hairdresser will be so carefully adjusting a little wisp, while smiling happily at the edifice with and for whom he has the ultimate responsibility of beautifying almost to the actress's ultimate potential. The star will happily bathe in their arse-licking ministrations and smile and giggle and relax and be fawned upon, waited on until the time comes to be ready for another take.

Meanwhile, during all this scampering and pampering you have been virtually alone and more than alone since alone can be nice, so more than alone … ignored. And that also is not a nice feeling. So you walk about, trying to get the attention of some underling who might just get you a coffee. Is there a chair to sit on, the actor's chair? No, there is no chair, not here. This is what you get paid for so don't complain. "Damn her! Lewd minx!" As he watches the little gang of smiling slaves he's as jealous as a dozen Othellos. On the first days, he tries his best without too much obvious genuflection to be friendly without being an unctuous, spittle-licking toerag. He was respectful, polite, but fell almost by accident, almost as a reflex action, into that ghastly role, taking that knee-bending attitude, flattering, praising her last film, even worse, praising the one before that, praising even her wonderful impersonation in the one before the penultimate and she, all the while smiling, thanking him, adding just a little comment. He, meanwhile, on his shiny knees even goes on to mention his personal knowledge of the actors she has worked with, even, yes, even in a moment of desperation, for god's sake trying to catch her attention by praising her lover who he caught a few years ago when they shared a dismal play together on the London stage. "Oh how kind of you," she said. She asked him nothing in return, nothing, no interest, no curiosity, nothing, not even for the form of it, to show, or pretend to show goodwill, a mere question. Nothing, he had turned into a spineless whimpering arse-licking toadying fawn and maybe, yes of course, that's just why she can't stand him, can't bear even the sight of him, can't bear even to cast her eyes on this piece of wobbling insecurity, as he digs into his grubby bag of compliments. That's how she made him feel and that's not a good feeling since he still had the child in him, which is true of most actors, and to be ignored is hurtful, painful and deeply unpleasant. However, from her point of view, what she probably finds as deeply unpleasant if not sickening is that need that seems to swell up in some actors when they meet her (like those grotesquely expanded throats on some strange birds) and is based more on a loathsome self-deprecating fear of people more powerful than yourself.

And it's that slobbering spittle-foamed blather that anyone would find utterly revolting, would they not? But surely, he thought, I don't present such a self-abasing neurotic cringer, do I? Of course not, but it's the terrifying scale of the imagination in some actors that they turn themselves into the most abject and vile beasts, and this same vivid imagination which is the source of all their creative powers and is responsible for their most exalted impersonations also turns on itself … alas. I suppose it's a double-edged sword!

He had admired her greatly in the past as one of those legends that appears once in a lifetime. She was once a beautiful actress who defied the cliché that beauty is only skin deep for she was an actress of exceptional power and men fell at her feet in droves. And so rejection from her, from her whom he admired above all was exceptionally painful and he had loathed that slaving reflex action in him that caused him to act like a paid servant ready to sacrifice himself whenever a star appeared. Was it his own struggle in the murky pits of the unknown, those great chasms where the low and wretched fight to make themselves visible? Like those pathetic fringe workers for whom fame and acknowledgement will only be an everlasting dream that they hope they will one day attain. Those that do attain it seem to move into the light, they glow, and when they walk on the street they seem to carry their own luminosity with them.

And as she strolls onto the set, she trails a train of nymphs, fairies and elves fanning the foul air in front of her strewing her path with lilies blowing on the bright flame of talent that the lady still possesses and who needs talent when the gods have made you so beautiful?

And he couldn't help but notice how those poor creatures who live in the penumbra of the great stars, those who perpetually grovel at their feet, swell with pride and indeed almost burst when the great star deigns to exchange some pleasantries with them. They soak up her attention and in that moment they are released from the dark dusty corner of the shadows they usually inhabit and beam as they bathe in her lustre, in her divine light. Rictus smiles fixed upon their faces, which are somehow always turned upwards, beaming all the more since the star hath given the bounty of her legendary fame, even for a few seconds to you, for a few precious unforgettable seconds you were her world. You were in her 'eye line'!

Of him they are thinking: She seems to be ignoring that peculiar man she is having to act with ... that awful man, that weird man, yes she seems not to be even talking to him, not even acknowledging him, not even beginning to share her time with him, between takes, and therefore are we not by this token, much, so much preferred than that horrid beast who our lovely, our adorable Madame is having to act with? Of course we are.

And so much empowered by this unspoken thought they gather and curdle around her and beam little glistening innocent smiles of pleasure and giggle at her quips and offer them back, cheeky little mini-snacks, little niblets of wit fed to the great goddess to nibble on.

He stands there impotently and observes all this and try as he may to ignore these feelings, they still come rushing in and the child in him feels wounded, neglected and even assaulted. It could be that what is totally unknown to her is that his child is a big one and needs attention from time to time. But now he has to deal with it and he will deal with this cold-blooded movie deity, this grotesque invention of others.

But come now, had he not seen all this before, feeling ignored, and cold-shouldered, even when he came with good will and hearty intentions. But his scenes were good according to the director and even confirmed by the producer and that was important and that was what he was being paid for. You get paid to be bored to death; paid to wait around while you sit chewing the hours; you get paid for the humiliation. That's what you get paid for.

She says nothing, for does she in fact have little to say? To her co-star she beams, smiles, flutters her eyelashes for he is a star as big if not bigger than her. But then again, why not? You stick to your own kind with whom you share the silver spotlight and it's not good to mix with the underlings, the horrid hoi polloi.

In spite of self-regard, the script is not only total crap, it's ninety-nine per cent vintage crap and these two, but these two great lights in the firmament have to put this horseshit in their mouths for weeks.

Now, it occurs to him that actors who are obliged for a fat pay cheque to speak and act garbage for weeks and even months will of course be totally unable to be unaffected by the dross that is continually invading their minds. Ah, yes, poor things, they will never have a chance to play the great roles, never a Lady Macbeth, a Miss Julie, a Blanche Dubois, a Mother Courage, a Cleopatra, no, never in their lives and how they must envy those who do, how they must squirm and pine and cast jealous and hungry eyes at those who can step onto that stage and without effort pour out the passions of their souls.

These thoughts evened out the odds so to speak and now he regarded her with no small amount of pity as he saw her still trapped in the scene, the same scene that he was gratefully now removed from, saw her still fiddling with the grim details, hour after hour and also thought of how a stage actor would by now have completed a rehearsal of the play and be purged, enlightened, transmogrified, and she poor, poor star was stuck in the fetid swamp of that dull scene.

Now, it was at the end of the day, a day in which he decided to ignore her, exchange no pleasantries, beyond the slimmest good mornings, when she suddenly smiled at him, thanked him for his effort and the great ice flow into which he had slowly been frozen, suddenly melted away … he was now bathing in that glorious power that shone so effortlessly out of her. He realised that his own pathetic insecurity was in no small way like one of those twisted mirrors you see in a fun fair which turns everything normal into something grotesque and ugly. Oh beware! He thanked her in return as it was the last scene they would have together, and now they were relating, talking to each other like fellow actors and her usual flotilla of dressers, and wardrobe and make-up sat some way off in the background like poor dull creatures. He went back to his hotel and lay in bed resolving in future not to be so beholden to the charity and kindness of others like a miserable beggar. In other words … wise up!

# 14.

# WAITING

He waited … he waited in his dressing room … he waited. He was called at the usual time and whisked to work; everything followed in an orderly pattern: getting up, washing, having a modest breakfast. The car was waiting outside to transport him to the studios. Unfortunately, as is all too familiar nowadays, the driver had sprayed the interior with a chemical 'fresh air', which made the car stink like an Essex whore, so he swiftly opened the window on his side of the car. The driver, like most British drivers made the usual small chat to pass the time: "Oh he was a real smashing bloke, no airs or graces", when reminiscing about other posteriors he had transported to the studios and "how lovely" they were and "what a sport" that one was and "how charming, a right lady", she was. What seemed to impress the driver was the very fact they talked to him, a mere underling. They were friendly and spoke to him and even confided little morsels of their lives to him, nothing meaty of course, just a few shreds, some crumbs thrown from their large and sumptuous tables for the eager dog driving them. For the actors it passed the time, it whiled away a rather tedious journey. These little nuggets which the driver, very proudly, passed back to him were the kind of well-worn dregs that the driver had been dining out on for years. The re-telling of them was a little glib. He imagined the driver in his local, entertaining his beery, foam-flecked mates all about his intimacy with the 'stars'. "What was he like?" "A diamond geezer, yeah." So in this way they passed the time as he watched the grim North London suburbs changing into fields and country lanes until they arrived at the studio.

Since he was actually called 'precautiously early', he'd pop into the worker's canteen where they served the most delicious industrial sausage which for some reason he found absolutely compelling and moreish, so he plonked it into a roll and smeared it with the contents of a filthy tube of ketchup which in the process of squeezing managed to get all over his fingers, and washed it down with a cup of sweet, brown tea. Then he entered his dressing room. The quiet zone. Here the actor sits and waits. He waits for his call and studies his lines, going over them again and again like a musician practising scales. Over and over again, until they become automatic. Then he tried some lines in a different manner, adding inflections, increasing volume on certain words, lowering the volume suggestively on others. The 'sides' for today's shoot were on the table so he worked from them, saving hoiking the whole script on your lap.

After a while, the monotony of the text and the jerkiness of the dialogue started to get to him and the lines therefore weren't adhering to his brain. They had no sticking power or resonance, no adhesive, so he had to learn by rote. After a while he put the pages down and had a break. He rolled a cigarette, drew deeply and immediately felt better. Then after a few more puffs, he brushed his teeth to clean his breath and excavate the bits of sausage stuck between them. He always carried a toothbrush to work – most important for an actor. He was wondering how long it might be before he was called when there was a knock on the door from the third assistant who asked him to go to make-up. Something to do and it passed the time and you felt that things were beginning to happen and the event for which you were called was drawing near.

He opened the door and saw two other actors who were in the process of being made up; he didn't recognise them but surmised they were playing the Russian 'heavies'. They exchanged enthusiastic 'Hi's', and then he sat down in his chair while the make-up artist strapped a bib round his neck to protect his costume from her travails. Just then a young woman of astounding beauty came in and 'Good Morning'd' everybody most cheerfully. She was tall and strong-limbed and possessed those qualities, so very English, that manifest themselves in a female of great classical and even cool beauty, clear skinned, flawless thick tawny hair and deep brown eyes. She was what one might call a Pre-Raphaelite beauty.

Her make-up person was cheerful and perky and not dissimilar to the driver who brought him in. With sponge in hand, happy to have the 'principal' under her fingertips at last, she uttered the usual banalities and was a model of charm and deference to the great star but was sure to mark your card if you, on the lower order of actors dared to show any sign of dissatisfaction or waywardness. Yes, beware, for these are the witnesses who delight in spreading every detail of your errant behaviour. These are the gossips, by whom the bacteria of rumours are heated up, multiplied and spread, and the rumours gather even more spiciness as they spread through the unwashed lugs of the 'fans'. Desperate, if not despicable fans who love you, but love feasting on you even more. But the stars love these 'attendants' for they are like your personal little part-time serv-ants, part of your never ending train of supporters and then stars having become used to the special attention, are also now addicted to it. The make-up of the lowly film actor is functional and to the purpose, while she saves the valuable oil of flattery and unctuousness for the star.

You dis-bib yourself and return to your room and wait, look at the lines again. Are they sink-ing in? Somewhat … a little more … so you go through them a few more times and gradually they are, through ruthless and tedious repetition, beginning to stick. You roll another fag. Boy that tastes good. Check your mobile. Nothing. So you run your few lines again, and this time without a fault. You take a piss. There's another knock on the door. It's the third assistant. Again. His face looks full of business and earnestness as he makes the rounds, doing all those things a third must do before showing himself to be so responsible and speedy that he may make it to second and then one day be a first but that takes real time and application. It's not like acting, when you might take someone off the street and lo and behold they turn out a reasonable performance. No, on their side of the camera you need real skill, and pains-takingly acquired knowledge. So the third says, "The director profoundly apologises but won't get to you before lunch." That's okay, something to do, a change of scenery and a delight for the gut. He takes off his costume, puts his street clothes on and goes back to the canteen.

Now there are two places to eat. One, naturally for the staff and crew and workers, and one for the upper strata. The actors, the stars, the film director and director of photography, and where you are given a menu and are served at your table. He did venture to peep into the posh place but didn't feel like sitting there on his own and so went back to the worker's canteen where he felt altogether more comfortable and waited for one of the small part players, or also-rans to join him later. He took a modest lunch since he wanted to be fighting fit for the afternoon's work. He ate his food slowly, eyeing the noisy happy gatherings at the other tables, and now regretted not being bold enough to just have gone with a magazine and sat in the place where proper actors sit and be waited on and at least enjoy some of the status of his posi-tion. So what if he sits alone, no matter, "just read your mag and enjoy the food." Here, he thought, "I'm alone anyway and what place is worse?" And then the thought occurred to him that maybe his colleagues, or rather his underlings went straight to the top-class restaurant and were enjoying themselves while he just sat, miserably in here!

He finally finished his modest lunch amidst the 'grips', the second and third assistants, the make-up and costume assistants, the focus puller, the sound engineer and carpenter, pulled himself up and walked to his dressing room, but on his way he passed the corridor that led to the hallowed dining room from which he had excluded himself. He just popped his head into the large high ceilinged room, just as if he was looking for a colleague, nothing more, just an outstretched neck look-ing busy, looking this way and that and then he caught sight of them. Those bloody Russian heav-ies sitting back and laughing like they were having a real neat time and what's more, they were sitting, would you believe, with that simply gorgeous young woman he had so admired. They were having fun, networking and chatting, while he had sat like a low-class mug in the worker's canteen! It merely turned out that they were sitting in the restaurant when she walked in, was alone, noticed that her co-star's table was full of company 'suits' so she made a quick decision to go slumming with the spare parts. "Now if I'd have been in there she would have course sat with me." "So look," he whined to himself "what my stupidity has let me in for." He turned his face away from their table and surveyed the other half of the room still keeping up his pathetic pretence and then withdrew. Rather pitiful and maybe an unfortunate characteristic to have, to downgrade yourself which was quite unnecessary since others will most happily do it for you. And maybe this same characteristic might be the reason that this quite well thought of actor had never really stepped into a stronger light … as if he didn't deserve it. "I won't do that again," he thought. "Oh no, I won't do that again. That's enough. That's the last time that stinking canteen sees me." But just as he was marching up the corridor, somewhat stiffened by his fresh resolve and studying all those black and white, glossy ten by eight photos of past stars, grinning happily out that lined the walls, he heard a voice calling him. He turned almost grateful for hearing his name being called, for at least being identified. It was the third assistant again, who rushed up to him breathless to tell him that he needn't rush from the restaurant, since they wouldn't be needing him directly after lunch since they were delayed and hadn't finished the 'reverses'. "Fine," Harry said, "Fine." "I was looking for you everywhere," the assistant went on " I thought you must have gone for a walk." "No, I was in the canteen." "Oh," the third replied, "I didn't think to look for you in there." By now he was walking purposefully back to his dressing room as if he had much to do, and the photos of the stars now seemed to stare back at him with a derisory smile. Oh bollix. But now he felt like a short nap. Just a short nap and then a run through of the lines. The canteen was fine. "Don't like a rich lunch, or even a chatty lunch when you've got work to do."

He went over the lines once more but for some reason they absolutely refused to stick to his brain! His brain, his beautiful, articulate, trained brain was rejecting them, as if spitting them back … uuggh! So he'd have a nap and try again but he was restless and tossed and turned in that empty room, so he got up, brushed his teeth. "Ahh, that's better," and then wanting to shake off the drowsiness he did fifty push-ups, which hyperventilated him and made him start to feel alive again and so before he started on the lines again he opened the window and stared outside. It was one of those drizzly wet days that felt as if nothing on this bloody mournful earth mattered, and his existence didn't matter at all that much and the work he was doing mattered even less. The agent said although it was only two or maybe three days work, it was a good cameo, playing one of those Russian tough guys who now seem mandatory for all thrillers since the shackles of Communism had been thrown off the

Soviet Union and they were now as greedy, selfish, grasping, immoral, disgusting, lying, cheating and thieving as anyone else, and maybe even better at it, having learned from ruthless masters.

Each era has its villains and he had played too many of the Russian ones and didn't have to work that hard on the accent any more. But the downside was that it seemed to prevent casting people seeing him in any other light; that's who he was, a villain, and particularly a Russian one, although sometimes a Nazi. No matter that he had played an exceedingly wide variety of characters on stage, to the industry he was a perfect, sullen, mean villain. "Yes, that," he had to admit to himself, "was how I am perceived by the world, as a cold, brutal sod" and that's no doubt was how he would be remembered. It saddened him and sometimes angered him to be thought of as a villain who simply liked hurting others. No matter, he did the roles well and was reasonably paid.

He rolled a cigarette and sucked deeply, and although he had just had a light lunch he was suffering pangs of hunger like he hadn't eaten for a week. His hunger was intense. It went right down to his boots, to his toes ... he was ravenous for life, for excitement, for passion, for titanic roles through which he could expel that deep well of emotion that lay curdling up inside him.

He stubbed the fag out and opened the window. Maybe he should just go onto the set, show his face get the 'atmos' a bit. But no, be patient, they'll call soon. Go over the lines a couple more times. Now the lines stayed, although not without a bit of effort but at least they did hang in there.

It's the worst crime in the acting world not to know your lines when on the set. Not to be word perfect, or D.L.P. as they say in the theatre. Dead letter perfect. Every take costs money and some-times a lot of money and not just in film stock, lights, props and the energy of the entire staff but the sheer cost of all those actors and stars who explode into triple time if they go over. And then there are those behind the scenes, the offices, the secretaries, publicists, writers, re-writers, so every slip you make, every stumble, every burble, every extra take kicks over another bundle of cash.

He went over his lines again and again … did them looking in the mirror, but the lines were tedi-ous and boring and too damp to ignite his spirit. He took another piss and then wondered whom he might call just to break the endless monotony. Call someone he had not called for a while, who might even appreciate a small chat. He actually felt lonely. Why on earth do these bastards have to call you so fucking early? He lay down again and this time he was feeling a little sleepy and half nodded off and was grateful for that. They must be having problems on the set. He raised himself, stretched and looked out the window. "Good god," he thought "it can't be getting dark already" but yes, it was just beginning to get that tawny autumn light ... the first pangs of the death of the day. He wished he had played Cyrano de Bergerac. He always loved that role, or Iago. He did see himself in that role as a cunning, dangerous Iago. Or even Othello, but those PC pigs snatched it away from the actor. Hey, who the fuck are they to tell actors what they may play or not play? Actors rarely if ever thought like that. It was only directors, or critics who thought like that, the ones that don't act and can't act and would never act and haven't got the guts to act that go on to tell actors what they may or may not play.

He rolled another fag and sucked it deep down. Then he went over his lines. Then he had another piss. He did some more press-ups. Then he rolled a fag, then he went over his lines, then he looked out the window, then he rolled another fag, then he went over his lines ... then ...

# 15.

# FUNNY HOW IT STARTS

O f course he had tried for many years to write and I mean, don't we all. Actors that is, try to write during those long fallow periods between jobs, euphemistically called resting in the old days, which movie stars might just do, but that word resting is almost as bad and as tainted as luvvie, which the media seem to have become so attached to in order to vilify actors for their emotional capacity and ability to bare their souls in public. Since quite rightly full-blooded and uninhibited emotion is the fuel of the performer and they certainly produce a lot of it sometimes as a biological product of their work. In fact audiences are drawn to those artists who can almost make a bonfire of their incendiary emotions.

You could say that the more actors are able to fully express their emotions the stronger the message in the play. In the same way that athletes develop muscular strength through practice and repetition, the better and more powerful they become. In the actor's case, an off-the-cuff remark that smacked just a little too much of unrestrained passion might inspire the most loathsome epithet of 'luvvie'.

Reflecting on it caused him to think that he didn't really mind being a luvvie since luvvies are generous, responsive, quick to take offence at unjust and cruel acts, don't kill beautiful wild animals for amusement or sport. One might say that luvvies love animals and protect wild things and campaign against barbarians who hunt, shoot and kill and who mix with other barbarians of that ilk. The opposite of luvvie I imagine would be a 'hatee' or barbarian. Barbarians ridicule luvvies and in fact hate and detest them for the ease with which they can express what they really feel. They can also do it without necessarily having to get drunk.

So, he was not resting, not really. He was struggling to think how he could give some shape to his life by actually writing about it.

He began to write a play. Not the first, since up to now he felt he had absolutely nothing of interest to say, and so he adapted the thoughts and words of others who had put them into novels and short stories. These he felt were so much more interesting than plays written straight for theatre. The stories he had chosen to adapt contained so much more of the tiny day-to-day detail that draws the reader in and builds a complete picture of society, and of course reveals the deep unconscious ramblings of the narrator. Plays were generally yards and yards of dialogue spat out at full metric force and if it was the verse of Molière it certainly had a musical excitement but sadly contemporary plays rarely had that exciting musical cadence.

But now he had decided to try to write an original play and the best place to start was with himself, for if one was a professor of anything, it was one's own personal, intimate private life. Do not painters do this? Study their physiognomy in a mirror and slowly and painstakingly analyse it and set it down. The painter uses the face that he has lived with for decades and slowly peels it away layer upon layer as he searches for that special defining feature.

In like manner, the neophyte writer began with himself and that's the best way, since of course, it has to be the truest, the simplest and the most revealing. And there again you know this person so intimately, so utterly thoroughly, so inescapably. However, when you begin to write, you find you haven't a clue where to start. Your pen is gripped and hovers over the page like a mosquito wondering where to land for the first bite. What should be the plot, what themes, what ideas, where should you start, how to begin? In every human being exists a wealth of material that would feed the engines of creation for over a hundred years, but unfortunately most beginners just don't seem to realise how valuable all that material is, how fundamental it was to your growth, to your action, to what makes you unique. But for some reason when you finally make that momentous decision to set it down, you suddenly feel dull, leaden, even unworthy. One feels far too unadventurous, too cowardly, too plain, too safe. So often a writer spends his entire life buried in the anuses of others more intrepid than themselves, analysing their every burp and belch and fart, researching every detail every crumb that drops from the table, from the grand feast that was their lives. They pin down every action of these courageous men and women who often fought against overwhelming odds, against the full weight of the tonnes of mediocrity stacked against them like so much shapeless blubber. And still they overcame all these obstacles and shifted the parameters of the world, pushed what was possible and what was acceptable up a few notches and revealed a new and fresh landscape.

As the painter seems to understand the structure

of the bony skull, the fleshy face, he also understands the movement beneath skin, the muscles, the ligaments of the tissue, the nerves, the stringy multiple connections upon which the face is pulled and stretched. So does the writer, so in fact do most writers peer beneath the outer action, to see from what depths they emanate, what memories wriggle, lurk and fester below the innocent gesture. It was the end of the Sixties and the beginning of the Seventies, the time when according to those romantically inclined, some strange alignment of the planets caused otherwise fairly normal people to behave as if drugged in some bacchanalian rite, to bare themselves, to rip off all conventions beginning with their clothes as if they were some kind of symbolic impediment to freedom.

All that had hitherto been jealously guarded and concealed was suddenly revealed as if by compulsion and as if by the very exposing of those dark areas a new dawn would arise. Not altogether convinced yet going with the flow, feeling the force of the surge that was sweeping the land he sat down to write only that which he knew, that which he had experienced: all those desires, all those torrid heated acts, and acts he would never breathe to any living soul, which for some reason he could write down and be prepared to expose them to the world since he could wear the mask of 'theatre'.

So he set down everything, all that was most profane, disgusting and infantile, a stream of filth, as if there was some deep reservoir within him of sewage that was just bursting to be expelled. Then he finished his script and in some way was proud. He felt lighter as he had unburdened himself. He made some copies of this turgid expulsion from his lower regions and gave it to a trusted actor friend. The friend gathered a few actors to read it together as a kind of test run and the actor told the writer that his friends could barely speak the words, could hardly, even in those 'liberated' times, let their sweet innocent mouths be soiled and defiled by those excremental words. The actor said 'well, yes, certainly it was different and even quite powerful in its way, but not for us.'

So the writer, almost anticipating this reaction and not being put out by it, not for a bit, just shoved the thing in a drawer, as one of those experiments one makes in one's early life, and forgets about it.

And then many months later, for no apparent reason, but just for its own sake, like one might doodle something or flick a few guitar strings, he felt like rearranging the words, make the words dance, play, work in a rhythm.

By some bizarre alchemical process the new order of words crept under the skin and revealed distant memories and most of all the fantasies.

Now the words had a form and dare one say it, a much more poetical structure and so no longer exposed his 'character' but 'revealed' it as if he was squeezing his thoughts through a sieve until the poisons were filtered out and the essence remained; some people might call it verse. The verse was the carapace, which kept the content intact. And so he changed the play except for one or two segments, which bore the cruder efforts of the first draft. But it was not only better, it was far better. Now by changing the order of the words and hoisting them to a rhythm it suddenly developed humour and irony. At least that is what he thought. More months passed and then one day, he decided that the time had surely come when he should stage it.

But now along with the cultural revolution, there was a sea change in theatres all over the world. We had seen strangely weird and marvellously inventive work from the four corners of the earth and our own simple, conventional staging seemed primitive if not actually banal. So he too must find a bold new way to express the text and the dynamic force of the actors. He went to work gathering around him some of the boldest, bravest and choicest actors he could find and it was so hard at first because he hadn't the faintest idea of how to stage it but he persevered, and it was made even harder since he decided that he would also play one of the principal roles. Somehow he knew that he had to. The story and the text had come out from deep within him. The play had been forged from his own blood, and guts, from his own sweat and angst, from his own pain and frustration and most of all from his own joy.

So while he auditioned many young men, none came even near to reading into it what was so vitally needed. Yes, he had not only to direct it but must play it, and in the end, thank God he did, for then he was wrapped in his own skin, in his own world, even if he still found hurdles to overcome. But in the end helped by such an extraordinary cast he felt so natural and it felt right.

It was one of those companies that he could fire with enthusiasm which when his own enthusiasm waned, when his doubts grew large, when his confidence faltered he could rely on them to fill the breach and so they did!! And how, with such assurance and such energy and being swept along by this confident burst of energy like on a great wave he was picked up and tossed onto the dry land.

Now the time came to put it on and since the writer-actor had not had the confidence to make the assumption that the play would be ready in four weeks, he of course could not take the risk and book a theatre. No, that would not be possible until he had tried it out, had tested it so to speak, in a dry run. So now he feverishly monitored all the small theatres and since it was the time of the Edinburgh Festival he rang up a theatre where he had already performed in previous years and begged them for a slot.

The only one left was at 11 p.m. The graveyard slot. This was the latest time possible at the Edinburgh Festival – that was all that was available; it would be absolutely fine. They would take the most undesirable slot and in some ways that would suit them.

His exhausted but devoted actors had to stay up, passing the time, going over the lines in the digs since the theatre was occupied except for the one lighting and dress rehearsal they had been allocated. They walked round the rowdy Grassmarket which was the large ancient square beneath Traverse Theatre but it was not until 10.30 p.m. that they were allowed into the stale dressing room, stale from the sweat and breath of all the other actors who had been playing all day. But then the theatre was finally theirs. At last they sat before the mirrors as all actors do and climbed into their sleek punkish costumes. "Beginners" was called, the time to stand by on that black stage. They started.

There is nothing in an actor's life to compare to the first time you speak your text to a live audience.

It's almost as if you're coming to life in front of them, building your personality cell by cell, as they watch. Since in watching they are also contributing. They are party to it as silent collaborators. So my dear and special audience, thank you.

# 16.

# STEVEN BERKOFF TALKS TO KIRK DOUGLAS

A while ago, I read something in *The Times* that was so wide of the mark, so brutish in observation that it ignited a small powder keg of anger inside me. I get this from time to time when nice middle class ladies, well educated, yet severely lacking in what we commoners might sentimentally designate as soul, degrade a piece of work. A piece of work so powerful, so generous in its passion that its message vibrates even today with as much resonance as ever.

The lady in question, who I have met and found utterly charming, regrettably wrote with disdain about one of my acting heroes, Kirk Douglas, in reference to his astonishing performance as Van

Gogh. She was reviewing an actual Van Gogh exhibition at the Royal Academy of Arts, which was displaying not only his paintings, but also his letters and other ephemera. From this she deduced that poor batty Van Gogh had moments of great lucidity and reason, which no one denies, and that his image was maligned by Kirk Douglas's 'ranting' performance. However, she is an art critic and a most readable one but hardly a drama critic. Nevertheless, as is my wont to defend our slender legion of acting heroes from the casual barbs of the media, I dashed a letter off to *The Times*, which the letters editor was good enough to print. I was proud to see my valiant attempt to defend our ancient hero in the national press. Since I would be even prouder, if the great Kirk could cast his eyes on it, I managed to locate his agent in Hollywood and forwarded a letter to him in the hope he would pass it on.

Many weeks later, by post, I received a simply glorious letter from Kirk himself. He thanked me profusely for taking his side, wrote briefly about the film and the pleasure of working with Anthony Quinn and of course playing Van Gogh into which role he poured his heart and soul. At the end of the letter he enclosed a small caricature of himself with the handwritten comment: "I'm an artist too!"

A letter from Kirk himself – it might just as well have been from the great God himself, the mighty Zeus sitting atop Mount Olympus, for is Beverly Hills not a suitable surrogate, where those glittering stars of the screen abide in their lofty perfumed palaces above the putrid carbon veil, which chokes the seething masses below?

As it so happens, a rare occasion comes when one is summoned to render some peripheral acting duty when the Gods of the screen descend the winding lush green avenues to the mighty temples of film, the studios. It is pure chance when your number is called and you must be ready and able and even more than that, totally and passionately willing to serve your masters, no matter what is asked of you, for you must never forget that it is for the stars, for whom you are merely background and furniture and regarded with as much affection by them as their props. Do not come with dazzled eyes, wet with thespian enthusiasm for their legendary performances, those roles that you have at least been permitted to see in your local popcorn stinking multiplex. They are simply not interested in your comments or your life or even your compliments. Just turn up and whatever you do don't try and engage in conversation with them for you represent everything they spent a lifetime escaping from. You are the hired help and since some of the luminaries may have dragged themselves heroically out of that snake pit they don't want to be reminded of it. Why? Because you still carry that slight whiff, that unmistakable odour of the low-life, the pond life, that stench of swamps and even, God forbid, of that loathsome sour aroma of struggle. Yucky! Spare them please, that unmistakable enthusiasm of the underdog for they hate that.

However, you will be deposited by van or people carrier, courtesy of the local Teamsters transport union at the studio. The limos are not for you so don't expect it. But oh, no you cannot take away the excitement of entering Paramount Studios through the big gate. Oh how thrilling that is even if now few films are made there for it is the age of TV sitcoms and commercials. But there it still sits, that magnificent gated entrance where the Gods of film make their entrance as they silently glide in, protected from vulgar glaucous eyes by tinted windows. You meanwhile have been bouncing up and down in your Teamster's union van where you have been entertained on the way by your colourful and amusing driver.

So having been summoned, I was transported, made-up, shaved, and deposited on the set. When I first came to Hollywood I was placed in what they call a 'honey wagon' since they were like cells in a honeycomb, four of five to a trailer and I was more than happy just to be there and sharing the very same oxygen as the 'greats.' Now I have my own trailer at least. You do your job and obey the director and please try to resist offering up suggestions or 'dialogue improvements'. That will get you into severe hot water as I have learned in the past to my cost. Let the director make the suggestions. The last thing they want is a smart-ass around.

The days passed and I did my duty to the best of my ability and on the last days my 'manager' who is like an agent but more involved and works with the actor's agent called me to say that Kirk Douglas would be most happy to meet me!! She had sent his agent my letter and now that I was actually here, Kirk offered to meet me, but only for fifteen or twenty minutes as he was preparing to go away for the weekend. Oh what joy! What a fevered delirium ran through my veins for I was going to meet the master, the God of acting, the mighty Apollo of the screen. The man who seldom gave anything but a flawless performance. One felt better just having seen him on screen, one felt enlivened, emboldened, inspired and most of all he helped to chip away at that horrible carapace that kept you trapped in your morbid, dull suburban life. Your very existence was better just for having been exposed to his explosive energy.

I was given the address and the time, 11 a.m. I would drive my hired car but just in case, even in the remotest case I was unable to locate the road I felt it better to hire a limo at $250 for two hours. I stepped into my shiny black Cadillac and sank into my soft creamy leather seats and we glided down Santa Monica Boulevard till we came to the outskirts of Beverly Hills on our left and threaded our way between the giant palms and slowly mounted the hills. The houses grew in magnificence, each surrounded by green lawns and sycamore trees. Some were Moorish in style, some ancient gothic or neocolonial. Most had friendly little signs by the gates: 'Armed Response'. We took a right and then a short way up was the number we were looking for. It was surprisingly modest in dimensions but elegant – a bungalow as would befit a senior citizen of generous years. The car pulled into the driveway and I got out and very gently rang the bell. I was five minutes early.

A middle-aged matronly lady opened the door, looked at me rather sternly and said, "You're a little too early. Mr Douglas is not ready for you yet." However, just at that very moment Kirk himself was coming out of the lounge with a young skull-capped man who it turns out was his rabbi on one of his weekly calls. I greeted the legend and apologised for being too early but he shook his head and said, "No, no it's fine," and introduced me to his rabbi who of course I greeted in Hebrew, just to warm things up a bit and then I was led into the lounge. He took the sofa and I an armchair facing him. Now I would have to say that it is the most curious feeling a man or woman can have when suddenly one comes face to face with a being that one might say has been immortalised through his screen image. And even more than this, one has grown up with, been inspired by, learned from, admired, been in awe of, until the actor through the sheer force of his personality has changed himself into a star as if some transformation had taken place on a molecular level.

And here he was before me, the legend and screen god and who like all screen gods can never ever age but be forever robust, and brimming with optimism. For there is something in Mr Douglas, something immutable and dare I say intrinsically pure that rendered his playing those great men so vivid.

I sat before the great deity and before me sat a gentle old man, a frail thin senior citizen, with a face whacked out of shape by a pernicious stroke, a face that was once as sculpted as Michelangelo's *David*. His blue eyes still had the fires of life in them though and with that inimitable tenacity he has even relearned to use his speech that was once lost. I spoke and told him of course of my great pleasure in seeing him. He responded by telling me how much it meant to him to read my humble letter defending him in *The Times*.

He wanted to meet me, he said, and thank me for standing up for his performance since that role, the role of Vincent Van Gogh, had meant so very much to him. He talked about visiting the little house in Arles where Van Gogh stayed and how hard he had worked to convey the anguish of a man who spent his life being rejected by all and sundry. He spoke of his friendship with Anthony Quinn and how much he had relied on and loved him and how very lonely he was since all his friends and allies were now literally *in* the stars. He added how he missed Burt Lancaster, Tony Curtis, Stanley Kubrick and most of all Billy Wilder. How he loved Olivier and enjoyed working with him so much and as he spoke the long legion of the greats passed by me like a procession of legends ascending slowly into the mist like one of those movie effects, when the heroes who served and died for us are seen marching into the clouds of history. I listened to him and enjoyed just watching him and relishing his joy. My camera was on the coffee table in front of us but for some reason I did not dare interrupt and ask him to let me take a shot.

I talked some more, since I had also to give him

a rest. I told him of my theatre work in London and what I was doing and he kept breaking in to say how much he respected theatre and especially those who kept it alive. When we talked of London, it seemed to revive him and he spoke fondly of his memories there and ever cheekily recounted how Vivien Leigh had a bit of an eye for him but wisely managed to restrain himself from the temptress. And then out of the blue he began singing to me! Of course it was one of his party numbers but nevertheless quite enchanting, for here was this 92-year-old geezer giving out in his croaky old voice a pretty good rendering of *Maybe it's because I'm a Londoner, that I love London toooown … Maybe it's because I'm a Londoner that I think of her wherever I go…* He went on right to the end of the ditty and it seemed to have charged some battery inside him, for he was beaming when he had finished, almost glowing.

It was natural that we got onto Israel and our experiences of that nation. He told me how he went before the grandees of Israel in Tel Aviv. He made a speech. This was many years ago. He made the speech in Hebrew, not the easiest language to remember. And at that very moment he launched into it: he had remembered it word for word after a half a century! Sometimes actors have this extraordinary capacity to recall important roles that they have played even if it was decades ago. There are a number of special roles that adhere to one's brain since they had become part of you like no other role ever could. He did the whole speech in perfect Hebrew. Perhaps he imagined that because I had greeted the departing rabbi in my scant few words of Hebrew I would be able to understand but I could not. The master had put me to shame.

Now it was time for me to leave since he had to get ready to depart to spend some time with his grandchildren in Santa Barbara. But before he got up he said, "Take a picture," and pointed at his housekeeper who had now become most benign. I showed her which button to press and I sat down on the sofa next to him. He was wearing blue trousers and a powder-blue cashmere sweater. I laid my arm gently around his shoulders and he laid his arm around mine. He said, "Now we're friends and we must always be friends." Under his soft sweater his body felt just a little frail. Suddenly he got to his feet and swiftly like a young man and guided me to the door. "Yes," I thought, "we must always be friends... Always."

# 17.

# TIME

He was unemployed, which wasn't too unusual and since he was used to it, he always managed to find an unending variety of activities to fill his time. He felt that time was like a beautiful garden that needed tending with the greatest care, to make use of the wonder of time and to create the most fantastic masterpieces since time would not be his forever. Time is a treasure given by the Almighty, to allow you to make something of the precious moments that you have been allotted on this planet.

His wife left each morning to go to her dance classes and as she went out how he envied her, her skills, her understanding of the science of the body that needed daily classes to help keep its perpetual motion, its extraordinary abilities, flexibility, rhythms, shape, and working with time itself just as a great sailing boat works with the wind.

As she left the tenement flat the walls seemed to close in on him since she kept time moving, lilting, happy, pleasant, giggly and so when she left she seemed to take all the elements with her. When she left the walls were bare, the room empty, where time stood still, waiting, waiting for what you were going to do with it. Time hung in the air, like it was a static thing waiting for you to shape it. He did envy her yes, for the ease in which she floated and fashioned herself around time and gave time meaning, made each moment precious, sweetened the moments with her movement and observations, her voice, wit, speech patterns. Now the flat was silent. He would once again shape the precious time and make the most astonishing patterns but not now. He stared out of the window and saw time making its unmistakable and inviolable march as the world heaved and bobbed and leaves flew through the autumn air, cats leapt from walls, and the horse was dragging the milk wagon, and the milkman took out gleaming white pints and delivered them onto doorsteps. The whole street was in its own rhythm of time but he, he was not, he, he might just as well be dead. He could have been on his deathbed since what energy he used was that of someone whose breaths were limited and could be counted.

This must not go on and he explained his grief to her one morning, his pain, his agony, his chagrin, his torture that he was not in rhythm with time but time was passing him by as surely as the tide of a river ebbs and flows only without you on it. And so she spoke softly to him, knowing his moods, knowing his frenzied moods when horrid shards of doubt cut through him, ripped him apart and left him helpless but she did know that once he was on the path there was no turning back. At least she did know that, that there was something in him that just had to be led, just helped to the first rung, the first note, the first step. Just lead him there since she knew him well. She was married to him and knew what a force could be unleashed by him when he would drive the very winds of time itself. And so she helped him, she led him to the water you might say. She helped untie the tethers that had kept the sails of his imagination tightly furled, released them and allow them to tumble down – soon he would capture the first soft exhalation of wind and his sails would billow out. She was sure of that.

She said, "I'm not rehearsing tomorrow, you can use the large room. Go in there and begin the play." She knew he had been wanting to do *Hamlet* for some time since this is the actor's dream, his goal, his ultimate ambition to pour this strange young man into your mind and body. To fuse with Hamlet, to become him, to play the instrument that is him.

But of course he had no company, no organisation, no administration, no theatre even, not even actors to play with, no dates to work towards, no costumes, no set, no vast reserves of wealth, no designers, no advisers. All he had was time. Time. And himself. But what a *him* he had, a special him that once started, once inspired would not let go, would not give up.

She knew in some instinctive way that wives have of sensing out the ill that troubles their husbands and rooting it out.

"Go to the large room," she said "and do some lines, go over some speeches, try it out, see how it feels. Do some blocking, play with him, with Hamlet, let the lines take you over." So the next morning he did. He had to. He could take it no longer and was on the point of collapse, of breakdown, and shuddering into meaningless entropy and casting all to the wind. The next morning, she gave him the keys and he unlocked the door to the church hall which his wife had been renting as a dance rehearsal space and as soon as he entered the hall there was a strange odour of expectation. A strange emptiness that was waiting. The air was pure and clear. It was even clean, clean and cool.

And once in the church hall, he imagined that he could feel the thousands upon thousands of bodies that had been squirming and twisting in there, in that space, and the old church walls seemed trusting and through the windows he could hear time pass, the big buses pass with their innocent load of old weary housewives going to only where housewives ever go and old men and school children, and the clip clop of metal-tipped heels of overweight ladies and schoolboys' shouts but all somehow filtered and softened.

He would start with a scene that he could act alone and there were many of them since Hamlet is often alone and enjoys his loneliness. There were chairs in the room and so he took one of them and placed it in the centre of the room and imagined that on the chair sat the villainous King Claudius, the man of no faith or ideals, no principles and no love. And for all that he has done, for all the crimes he has committed, a small sliver of regret has penetrated like a worm into his brain and he is trying to pray but cannot seem to get that feeling of release when saying those precious words, the words that are like hot sparks that can set one alight in a passionate fury of repentance and with repentance would come salvation. But he cannot be lit. He is damp and wretched, sweaty, dank with loathsome sin. He can only kneel and pray. Hamlet sees him from a doorway, sees this beast praying and now this is the chance to end him once and for all.

"Yes, this will be a good scene to start with," he thought. "I will imagine the king kneeling in front of his chair. I will slowly approach: 'Now I will do it pat, now he is a praying and so I am revenged!!'"

In the old cold city of Edinburgh he began the first attempts to create the character of Hamlet. He said the lines and they felt good. He was acting and more, he was filling himself with Hamlet. He was Hamlet while outside the buses were sliding their merry way to Stockbridge and in a church hall a lone, miserable man was for some unearthly reason speaking the lines to a play that had been written over four hundred years ago.

Now he was feeling better, he was feeling even good. His voice was clear, strident, penetrating, with a hard bright tenor tone. He ran through the entire scene over and over again until his older, lachrymose self was being driven out and an alert, revengeful, passionate man with no uncertainty was filling up his body.

He said the lines over and over. Repeated the words, addressed the invisible king. It felt as if the words carried little bolts of electricity. And the more he did them, the more his battery was charged and now he was approaching the kingdom of Hamlet where the actor would once again reign supreme. He was elated, relieved, felt purged. Felt that he had discharged some infernal weight of debris that had somehow lodged in his craw.

He went home and told his wife how much better he felt and that he would do this every day. And now he had a goal. Now he was flowing with time, not simply passing it, wasting it, wishing it gone. Not now. While his sails were beginning to billow in the wind which slowly nudged him forward he knew that now he must have a crew since Hamlet is a play with many parts and each part is vital to the whole. It is not a one-man show with a bunch of underlings as if they are there merely to feed the star the lines even if this is the way it has been performed for many years on our dank shores.

He was back in London and talked to some of his acting colleagues, well at least to two of them, and now that he had started to recharge his battery his sails were billowing. And now that his heart was beating strongly he was able to convince them that this journey would be a special one and he fired them with some of his own enthusiasm. So rather than just himself playing Hamlet exploring the kingdom of Elsinore, he would be accompanied by two of his intrepid co-travellers. Matthew would play King Claudius, and Barry, Laertes and between them they would at first share the other roles. Testing them out; finding out their routes and moves, the characters and their nature and once we had done this, once they had explored the whole terrain, they would, slowly and with great care bring in one more performer: first Gertrude, who was played by Linda. Now they were four and they continued this way until they added a Horatio, who was Garry and then an Ophelia who was Chloe, then Sally. And then Wolf came to do the Ghost. And so the company grew bit by bit until it seemed that it was an entity that just came into being like a birth; like something so natural and easy, and then he knew two splendid actors who were in fact twin brothers David and Tony and they would be Rosencrantz and Guildenstern.

So all these quite wonderful actors came together as if to create a family, and they became a family that would stay together for years with only an occasional member leaving and being swiftly replaced and they all loved the project and even loved each other and lived to rehearse and come to the studio which was now a church hall in Holborn. This church hall had a floor which was demarcated by white lines like a basketball court. As it so happens, ideas most often come when you least expect them and so these lines, these wonderful white lines became like architect's lines in a drawing of a building. So they were pathways, the walls of the castle, even the turrets. They had the castle on their very floor which they could summon up in seconds and just as quickly dissolve – oh how wonderful to summon up the mysteries of the imagination so easily and there it was; just in front of them.

How to bring the actors on and off stage was simply solved – they would never leave the stage. They would be an orchestra reflecting on the events as they unfurled on stage and comment and often join in. An orchestra and as such were dressed in beautiful black and white dress suits with smart tails and starched shirts and how elegant they looked.

And then, one day they opened in a church hall in Edinburgh at festival time and put the audience in seats on four sides of their performance. And they couldn't even shelter in front of a harsh light since there were none and so they played in a general light. You could not escape from the audience for a second. And then one day, the player Hamlet's wife came, the woman who had set the whole thing in motion many months before, but he could not see her. To do this work the actor has to *be* Hamlet or Claudius or Horatio or Ophelia. He knew that his wife was in because as he moved round the stage he could see her shoes peeping out. His wife's shoes, but he concentrated until the audience became merely a blur to him.

And so the company came together and everybody was so happy because they all felt that they were presenting something just a little bit special and this was confirmed by the audience and their splendid reactions. Then as things grow, as actions produce reactions and as energy inspires energy, they found a man who wished to tour the play throughout Europe and so they did. They took their wonderful company which now included a musician to the great theatres of Europe and everywhere they went they were acclaimed and the company explored this great and majestic continent, travelling from Dusseldorf to Frankfurt, Amsterdam, Rotterdam, The Hague, Basle, and finally in Paris at the Théâtre du Rond-Point where the great Jean-Louis Barrault, the finest actor-manager in France, had his company.

They played for two long weeks in Paris for the great genius Jean-Louis Barrault and what on this earth could have been a better way to finish their great tour. The company had been playing *Hamlet* on and off for three years. He even wrote a book about it. Now it was over. Time passed beautifully and they sailed upon it like a ship in full sail and banners fluttering. And they never forgot it.

# THE ACTOR'S LIFE

What is this life, this dreary endless wait…
Will they use me or not? We'll let you know,
They liked you, the ever hopeful agent spake,
To be or not to be, the madman's role.

So what, so what … you chose this life, this pain,
To twiddle your thumbs, drive in the slow lane,
Chatter with some lost and forlorn dame,
Fantasise the parts you never played.

It passes well the time, the endless game,
I'd like to play Macbeth, I will one day,
And woo the audience to love me so,
And be impressed by my iambic flow.

And smile and hold each other's sweaty palms,
Be so amazed by dazzling vocal skills,

That I did practise daily on the rack,
Of unemployment, while idiots had their stomach filled.

But no, I don't need admiration's gaze,
Not just for that, am I a willing slave
But to give, to strive, to earn my pay,
By illuminating Shakespeare's page.

But then I worked and slaved on ancient texts,
And learned great speeches that I might perform,
In front of darkened mouths of theatres, tests,
To show you're fit to earn your grain of corn.

You might hold a spear or play the fool,
Be given vapid, stupid roles to learn
While waiting for the work that feeds your soul,
For that my heart with passion burns.

The audience with wide and hungry eyes,
Desire magic, fury, great panache,
Admire the great, the noble and the kings,
While your slim part stands quivering in the wings.

§

Before your entrance comes, the tannoy calls,
You step so swiftly down the endless stairs
And now you hear the cue, your footstep falls,

Onto the retinas of a thousand stares.

"What now endure ... who is this dreary soul,
Another player yet to confuse our minds?
What is his purpose? Oh he is so drôle,
Oh sometimes just how heavy weighs the time.

How long before the interval relieves
This tedious fellow from his dreary act?
Oh babble on you piece of worthless meat,
Meanwhile I think I'll take a quiet nap!"

It's going well and better than I hoped,
The words are springing out and hitting home,
The audience though are restless, stupid drones,
When they should be alert to this great poem.

A coughing starts, erupting in the stalls,
Which like a forest fire throws its sparks
On other coughers who had bravely willed
Their coughs in with a thumping heart.

But now the star has left hallowed stage,
They feel more free to discharge straining barks,
Which stride like eager pups from owners' mouths,
Five hundred fed-up people in the dark.

But still the lonely small-part player strives,

To organise his tiny well-learned text,
Between the ripping sounds, his precious lines
Are layered with splutter, choke and stinking breath.

The lights go down, the curtain slowly falls,
And actors warble merrily their tales,
Oh how this line went well and that line palled,
And what a laugh was got while others failed.

§

And so the stars stared proud back at themselves,
Their make-up – enhanced features, they explored,
Oh yes my teeth are white as pearl seashells,
When lips are painted crimson, sharp and raw.

Oh how my slack cheeks now are sculptured rock,
With shading to enhance the thinning hair,
And eyebrows darkened, lined to bravely lock
My watery eyes into a hero's stare!

But me, the fill-in, plaster for the play,
Who tries to link the frail plot to make sense,
Up high with other splinters from the stage,
We humbly wait for act two to commence.

Some tea, a slow-dragged fag, a quick call home,
Make-up adjusted for the final scenes,

For those less occupied, and minds that roam,
Some scrabble eats the minutes till the tannoy screams.

"On stage, stand by," we swiftly leap downstairs,
The door is quietly opened on the deck,
The stage where Hamlet invites limpid stares,
Already tender-hearted cheeks are wet.

Yes we are here to swell a scene or two,
A graveyard priest, a small oration there,
Not gabble, but make sense, the audience knew,
That we were just spare spuds inside the stew.

So they can shut down their attention span
And give the brain a well-deserved rest,
Consult the watch, programme now a fan,
And dinner thoughts, yes, sushi may be best.

At last, at last, the ghastly show is done,
The punters bravely clap with sheer relief,
To get outside and stretch their pinioned bones,
"Ah well, I saw the bloody thing, now... fish or beef?!"

§

The actors string themselves together once again.
"Oh no, enough already, you've had your claps."
The star is bowing wanly, oh so 'drained',

For having bared his soul to all us chaps.

And now he bows down deeply, as if so moved,
By such a mild response from that shaggy lot,
11 p.m.'s last order or we will lose,
The table at the Ivy, we'll have to trot!

"No more! We're getting out of here, let's fly,
Oh darling we're running a trifle late,
I thought the bugger would never die,
Of course I loved it, those bits when I was awake!"

Another night is over for the prince,
Who washes off his makeup and the sweat,
Next door Gertrude and Ophelia whine,
Exchanging notes on how 'their' scene's a mess!

Of how Hamlet did this and how he did that,
And he used them like two broken dolls,
Venting his raging passion while his spit,
Just landed on their faces like hot fat!

Never mind and sod it for theatre's sake …
We have our weekly wage … the part's a prize,
My boyfriend shags me faithfully twice a week,
No more than that in case his wife gets wise.

The play is over, put once more to bed,

The pieces reassembled every night,
Just like a jigsaw puzzle that you rend
And throw back in its box and out of sight.

But, this human, living jigsaw thrives,
And links its pieces smartly like a clock,
You know the time it starts and when it dies,
Just wind it up once more, and hey, tic-toc!

§

It should get smoother running every night,
An actor lets the lines sink in his soul,
And plucks new cunning readings to delight
The audience, that often sit there like glum ghouls.

But no, not all, for some this is the treat,
A feast of Shakespeare, punning wit and verse,
To trick the ear as actors mark the beat,
They smartly giggle as those naughty couplets burst.

Oh, how jolly, clever, witty, smart and sage ...
When Hamlet mocks the vile usurping king,
And drives the cunning villain in a rage,
As barbéd rhyming metres leave their sting ...

And on and on, another night flies past,
The curtain drops, the stories rise and fall,

They clap, old gossip told and actors laugh,
We wash the make-up off and mobiles call.

It's like… it's like another day has passed,
Oh bliss, oh joy, I got through yet another,
My mind retained the clues that come so fast,
And now we have sweet freedom till the morrow.

But now, oh now, like dogs let off a leash,
So sweetly freedom floods into our veins,
We conquered yet again this ancient beast,
And now we play, yes, now the actors feast.

Will she meet me backstage now, I hope?
For now this shred of evening that is left,
Must fulfil my much depleted soul,
The first drink after work's always the best!

"Oh darling, you were fab tonight, straight up."
A kiss, her cheek is autumn chilled smells sweet,
"You were so brill, and where we going to sup?"
"Joe Allen's good," I didn't miss a beat.

§

"Really?" I did feel better, yes, tonight.
The lines they seemed to snap out of my mouth,
Like arrows, swift and piercing, straight in flight,

Each night is different of that I have no doubt.

"Oh yaa! It's different, that's for sure, OK?"
"But tell me darling was I at my best?"
"Of course, that's what I mean, you caught the play,
Oh god, I'm dying for some chicken breast!"

So down the nimble stairs we trot all keen,
Observe the posters pinned like flags of state,
That advertise the plays that died last week,
"Table for two, yes, smoking if that's OK."

But oh, your fellow actors are out of joint,
As if they're curling slightly at the edge,
Like boredom starts to seep in and it stales,
Their once enthusiastic thespians' breath.

"A carafe of your best, house wine, I mean,
A Caesar salad and that great bean soup,
A burger, medium rare and that's for me,
The soup's as thick as tar and makes you poop!"

"For madam, breast of chicken and French fries,
There's Michael Gambon, an actor now well sought
He's doing the L.A. bit I see these days
It's better than earning twopence at the Court!"

"Oh isn't that the critic Nick de Jong?

He's grinning now just like he's skinned a cat,
He's so appealing when his claws are out,
And tears the throat out of some turgid crap."

"There's Alec MaCowan, isn't he looking well?
His profile seems to slice the very air,
And if his words were fruit, they'd be so sweet,
Of all the actors, I think he was most rare."

§

The wine is quaffed and hungry mouths devour,
While eyes explore the table's eager guests,
Few actors now, more musicals inspire
The twirling dancers to Joe Allen's nest.

We pay, and snake between the table's roar,
And smile at one, at others flick a wave,
The night ensnares us in its carbon shawl,
A taxi hailed and through the night we sail.

But yet the night's not over, still the blood,
Is heated by the stage's fierce demands,
But slowly, slowly does the soul give up,
Those precious pearls of freedom that it won.

And now the memory of that victory fades,
As daily life and matters drive away,

The glorious conquest of your escapade,
And makes us smell the sourness of the day.

We wake, I fill the kettle, light the stove,
Pour green tea in the strainer, organic too,
I cut two slices from a dark brown loaf,
And grill it blackly while the kettle boos.

There was a bakery, end of Berwick street,
Whose bread was crunchy and dark-hued,
Next door a deli sliced smoked salmon, neat,
And pickled cucumbers were munchy Jews.

And down the market stalls, in summer's heat,
I'd buy the softest avocado pears,
And button mushrooms, tender as soft teats,
Fat red tomatoes, chicory, picked with care.

Oh how I loved that coloured fruit-filled stroll,
Amongst the slush of battered spinach leaves,
Crushed grapes that fallen from the stalls,
Lay split, and slithery, spewing out their seed.

§

My shopping bag was full, the red bus leaps,
Some pounds still stuffed in wallet's soft caress,
How lovely to get wages every week,

The toast is crisp and salmon drapes its breast.

A tray is carried to the basement room,
"How sweet you are" the sleepy magpie sings,
Oh lovely, gurgle, bite, she lifts the gloom,
From the grey-sky'd, heavy morning London scene.

She goes, she was my schooner of the night,
That sailed me through my darkness and despair,
I clung to my heaving craft with all my might,
And safely reached the shores with loving care.

There's something special in the honey'd sleep,
Betwixt a lover and his sweetest miss,
Incomparable and endless bliss,
But then in youth, too often passion shrieks.

But as the heart grows wiser, knowledge soars,
And renders flesh and spirit in one grip,
For lust, when passing leaves a deadly bore,
Since true love's pleasures are just infinite.

Two pulsing bodies sweetly move as one,
An awesome awareness of the joy of this,
Makes love, the only eventual outcome,
Where you'll find heaven, even in a kiss.

But now the flat is cold, and dull, remote,

Absent of the glow that gave it warmth,
Slouch in a bath and feed the mewing cat,
And scuttle down the road like a timid rat.

The hours are on your side but only just,
Until the large hand slowly slides past twelve,
And then you start to watch the minutes pass,
And thus begins the slow descent to hell.

§

A mind in hell is not a pleasant place,
A little demon robs you of peace and calm,
You even dream of running off the stage
To sanctuary, comfort and soothing balm.

But that's the usual angst before the stage,
Expectation with a twitch of fear,
But in the dressing room with all your mates,
Their lively chatter puts you more in gear.

Their energy and strength inspires yours,
Their love is like a life-line that you seize,
And you give them, your love's returned,
Although you feel your courage in your knees.

But soon this will be over and our group,
That was so close and intimate today,

Living for each other's words to hook
Our own words to and make the play.

We smell each other's breath and feel the sweat,
Our very lives depend upon each soul,
And so in such a strong and keen embrace,
We hold each other up, and that's our role.

Our role on stage and then again in life,
Don't be a thief and steal his precious laugh,
Because the actor's skill is like a light,
That will expose a grubby pirate's craft.

But be all generous and learn from all,
Respect their heartfelt talents, conflicts, end!
You will shine in their reflected glow,
And let your final curtain fall, with friends!

§